Corsair
KD431

THE TIME-CAPSULE FIGHTER

Corsair
KD431

DAVID MORRIS

SUTTON PUBLISHING
in association with

FLEET AIR ARM
MUSEUM

FLY NAVY

First published in 2006 by
Sutton Publishing Limited · Phoenix Mill
Thrupp · Stroud · Gloucestershire · GL5 2BU
in association with the Fleet Air Arm Museum

British Library Cataloguing in Publication Data
A catalogue record for this book is available from the British Library.

ISBN 0-7509-4305-X

Above: Corsair KD431: roll-out day, 9 August 2005.
Half title page: Corsair KD431, the last known Fleet Air Arm Corsair to survive in its original
condition. It was saved from extinction by this project. *(FAAM)*

Designed by Glad Stockdale.

Typeset in 10/13pt Sabon.
Typesetting and origination by
Sutton Publishing Limited.
Printed in Great Britain by
J.H. Haynes & Co. Ltd, Sparkford.

Contents

For Tony Mitchell,
to whom KD431 meant so much,
and to whom I owe such a great deal.

Acknowledgements

With thanks to all of those who assisted this project with help, information, details, equipment, support or belief. The Director and the Trustees of the Fleet Air Arm Museum; the Fleet Air Arm Museum Archive; the Royal Navy; Naval Secretary, Royal Naval Photographic Section (Yeovilton); Goodyear Tire & Rubber Company Collection, University of Akron Archives; Vought Aircraft Industries Inc; Vought Heritage Foundation; Aircraft Braking Systems Corporation; Cranfield University Archives; Smithsonian National Air & Space Museum; Glass-aid UK Ltd; Refinish Systems Ltd, Yeovil, UK; Gramos Ltd, UK; Townsend Bearings Ltd, Bridport, UK; the Imperial War Museum, Duxford; Woodall Industries, Detroit; *Aeroplane Monthly* magazine; *Air Pictorial* magazine; *Flypast* magazine; The National Archive (USA); Harry Dempsey Graphics; Dave O'Brien Photography; Nigel Cheffers-Heard Photography.

Steve Paschen, John Miller, Lynnc M. Warne, Pete Elizondo, John Harrington, Will Lee, Graham Mottram, Julia Hodson, Jerry Shore, Jan Keohane, Catherine Rounsfell, Ron Twamley, Bob Beers, Barbara Grimes, Wendy Coble, Barry Zerby, Mark Evans, Larry Webster, Rob Ball, Mike Furline, Martin Hale, Richard Able, Richard Laird, Richard Barlow, William Gibbs, Barry Cross, Garry Bussell, Mick Burrow, Ray Sturtivant, Judy Carr, John Fricker FRAeS, James Halley MBE, Norman Pratlett, Dave O'Brien, Bill Fisher, Russ Snadden, Peter Schofield, Chris Knapp, Nick Hauprich, Jonathan Coombes, Martin Hale, Malcolm Lowe, Peter R. March, Harry Dempsey, Cdr R.C. Hay DSO, DSC, Tony Mitchell, Stan Deeley, John Taylor, Douglas Buchanan, John Morton, Eric Beechinor, John Foulkes, Peter Jupe, Peter Lovegrove, Chris Clark, Cdr Lionel Hooke, Elizabeth Horsford, Ursula Bagnall, Hubert Hartley, Lavinia Woodbine-Parish, Ken Ellis, Melvyn Hiscock, John Lane, Gary Kohs and Nigel Cheffers-Heard.

Special thanks to the Aircraft Restoration and Conservation Team at the Fleet Air Arm Museum, without whose support, patience and determination this project would not have happened; and to Jonathan Falconer, Jane Hutchings, Bow Watkinson and Glad Stockdale at Sutton Publishing.

Thanks also to the former members of the Historic Aircraft Preservation Society, whose far-sighted approach during the early days of aircraft preservation enabled KD431 to be placed with the Fleet Air Arm Museum.

ABBREVIATIONS

ATA	Air Transport Auxiliary
c.g.	centre of gravity
CAFO	Confidential Admiralty Fleet Order
CO	Commanding Officer
CPO	Chief Petty Officer
FAA	Fleet Air Arm
FAAM	Fleet Air Arm Museum
FDO	Flight Deck Officer
FONAS	Flag Officer Naval Air Stations
NAS	Naval Air Squadron
RNAY	Royal Navy Aircraft Yard
SNAW	School of Naval Air Warfare
Sqn	Squadron
USMC	United States Marine Corps

METRIC EQUIVALENTS

Corsair KD431 was manufactured at a time when metric measurements were not used by Great Britain and the USA. Consequently all of the measurements in this book are given in the old Imperial standard. Below is a list of some of the more common conversions.

Imperial	Metric
1in	2.54cm
1ft	30.48cm
1 ounce (oz)	28.35g
1lb	0.4536kg
1 ton	1.016 tonnes
1 mile	1.6093km
1 pint	0.568 litre
1gal	4.5461 litres
100mph	160km/h

Preface

THE START OF A REMARKABLE PROJECT

For many years a story had been recounted by various people, telling how Vought Corsair KD431 had been flown back to England from Ceylon at the end of the Second World War. This explained (apparently) how the Corsair came to exist in the Fleet Air Arm Museum (FAAM) in postwar years as the last surviving example of its type in Great Britain.

But how much of this story was accurate, and was KD431 really the aircraft that made such an epic journey? These questions, combined with a

From the outset, the Corsair KD431 project looked interesting, challenging and exciting. By completion we had discovered many extraordinary details, stories and coincidences surrounding the aircraft. *(FAAM)*

growing suspicion that beneath a thin film of paint there lay a substantially more original Second World War aircraft than most people realised, formed the basis for this remarkable project.

To understand the aircraft fully, and unravel the myths and truths surrounding it, required an enormous research task. That would be followed by thousands of hours of painstaking detail work, to achieve what initially seemed an impossible goal. The skill and patience of all those concerned was eventually rewarded, but not necessarily with the results expected or, at times, wished for.

As a result, probably the last truly original Corsair fighter in existence was revealed; one of very few Second World War aircraft in such original condition.

This book records the project in great detail, and is deliberately intended to cater for a wide range of interests and needs, whether technical, detailed or historical. It also includes a few unexpected surprises regarding KD431's history.

David Morris, the author. *(FAAM)*

Chapter One

The '**Ensign Eliminator**'

The Chance Vought F4U Corsair

If there was one vice that plagued the Corsair throughout its life, then it was the huge amounts of torque produced by the big R2800 radial engine at low speeds. If an inexperienced pilot jammed the throttle to the firewall on take-off, the torque could easily twist the aircraft on to its back and ruin the pilot's afternoon. In the US Navy this tendency soon earned the Corsair the nickname 'Ensign Eliminator'.

This book is not a definitive history of the Corsair aircraft; many other authoritative texts do that job very well. It is a detailed history of one particular Corsair, and what we can understand from studying it closely. However, it would be wrong not to include a potted history of the type and a brief catalogue of interesting facts, to set the scene for those less familiar with the aircraft (see box).

VOUGHT AIRCRAFT CORPORATION

The development of the Vought Aircraft Corporation:

1917   Lewis and Vought Corporation formed
1922   Chance Vought Corporation formed
1929   Chance Vought joined with Boeing aircraft, Hamilton Standard, Pratt & Whitney and United Airlines to form United Aircraft and Transport Corporation
1935   Chance Vought Aircraft, Sikorsky Aircraft, Pratt & Whitney and Hamilton Standard became subsidiaries of United Aircraft Corporation
1939   Chance Vought Aircraft and Sikorsky Aircraft joined to create Vought-Sikorsky, a division of United Aircraft Corporation
1943   Chance Vought and Sikorsky Aircraft became separate divisions of United Aircraft Corporation
1948   Chance Vought moved its base to Dallas, Texas
1961   Chance Vought became a division of the LTV Corporation

A full history of each stage in the company's development is an in-depth subject in itself, and beyond the scope of this book. This list does, however, help to make sense of how the company was named (or with whom it was associated) at any given period; often an area of confusion. For the purposes of this book, and to keep references simple, the Vought Corporation will be used where the F4U Corsair is concerned.

THE BIRTH OF THE F4U

The name Corsair could not have been more appropriate for this powerful and formidable naval fighting machine. Its menacing form, plus its speed and firepower, relate it to the fears associated with piracy and hostile actions on the high seas, where the title originated.

The Vought Corporation had previously given the name to a biplane designed in the late 1920s and used very successfully in a variety of roles by the United States Navy between 1927 and 1942.

With a hard day's flying at an end, deck-crews aboard HMS *Illustrious* in the Far East manhandle the enormous Corsair fighters onto lifts to take the aircraft safely below, 1944. A long night of servicing and repair work is about to begin. *(FAAM)*

The concept of a totally new, high-speed, shipborne monoplane fighter arose in February 1938. Vought's engineering and design team, led by Rex B. Biesel, rose to the challenge set by the US Navy, and had two worthy designs approved for consideration by April that same year. Both designs, given the factory designations V-166A and V-166B, used the air-cooled radial engines readily available from the Pratt & Whitney Engine Company of East Hartford, Connecticut, USA. This choice of engine reflected the US Navy's preference for large radial-engined aircraft, with which it was both comfortable and familiar.

The V-166B was to have the mighty Pratt & Whitney XR 2800 Double Wasp engine. At 1,850hp this new engine was the most powerful aircraft piston engine available for the project. By the final stages of Corsair development Pratt & Whitney had taken the power output of this engine through the 2,000hp barrier to 2,300hp.

Such an engine required an extremely large propeller to take full advantage of all of this power, and the largest available unit was provided by American propeller manufacturer Hamilton-Standard, also of East Hartford, Connecticut. The three-bladed propeller was of 13ft 4in diameter, and was the largest propeller unit fitted to a single-engine aircraft at that time. This brought about the conflicting needs to maintain sufficient ground clearance for the propeller, yet retain short undercarriage legs for strength and stability. The solution to this design dilemma was the characteristic gull-wing configuration that became such a distinctive feature of the F4U series Corsair. This configuration also had the advantages of conveniently enhancing the pilot's over-wing view and giving a lower drag factor.

The Vought Corsair O2U-1 scout/observation aircraft. The Vought Aircraft Company had previously used the name Corsair for a landplane and seaplane aircraft designed for the US Navy in the 1920s. (Vought Aircraft Industries)

The prototype XF4U-1, from which one of the most powerful fighter aircraft of the Second World War was developed. Note the fuselage-mounted machine-guns in the upper engine cowlings and the early 'bird-cage'-style cockpit canopy. Note also that, at this early development stage, the pilot is seated nearer to the aircraft's nose than on final production models. *(Vought Aircraft Industries)*

Enthused by the concept, the US Navy issued a contract to Vought on 11 June 1938 for the production of a prototype, officially designated XF4U-1. In just eight months, by 10 February 1939, a full-scale mock-up had been produced and windtunnel tests had been carried out. As if this remarkable achievement was not impressive enough, the maiden flight of the first prototype Corsair took place on 29 May 1940, a mere sixteen months (473 days) later.

The US Navy had its own experimental aircraft engineering establishment, and together with the Vought Corporation it developed a new technique for spot-welding aluminium sheets to airframes. The new technology (used in conjunction with the more familiar riveted skinning) produced an immensely strong fuselage structure and also reduced construction time.

Most aircraft are designed with rearward-pointing exhausts, to aid streamlining and to enable them to benefit from the small amount of rearward thrust created by the exhaust gases (marginal in most cases). However, the Corsair was the first fighter aircraft to incorporate an exhaust system specifically designed and routed (from prototype stage) to exploit this small extra source of power.

The Corsair's fifth test flight ended in a near-disastrous crash landing that would have destroyed many lesser aircraft. Substantial damage to its wing, tail, fuselage underside and engine areas was rectified within three months, testifying to the quality of Vought design and engineering.

Further proof of design and capability was provided when the Corsair blasted through the 400mph barrier (one reference indicates a date of October 1940). It was the first American-built aircraft to do so, refuting the US Army view that fast aircraft had to have in-line rather than radial engines.

At first glance the prototype Corsair looks little different from the production models, but nearly 300 major and more than 3,000 minor modifications were incorporated into the design during the aircraft's production span.

Intended as a fighter, its light bombing capabilities were considered and made use of from the initial stages, though in a somewhat novel manner initially. Within the wings of the prototype were compartments capable of carrying twenty small 5lb bomblets (ten per wing). These midget bombs were intended as anti-aircraft weapons, to be released from above on to formations of enemy bombers. This idea was abandoned before full

The unmistakable frontal profile of the Corsair. The use of the gull-wing configuration to raise the engine and provide ground clearance for the propeller, while keeping the undercarriage short and strong, is very clearly portrayed here. However, pilots' needs, such as a clear forward view for take-off and landing, seem to have been of secondary importance. *(FAAM)*

production began, but the Corsair became a very capable strike bomber when fitted with more conventionally mounted bombs and rockets. The original machine-gun armament comprised two 0.303in Browning guns mounted in the upper engine cowling, synchronised to fire between the propeller blades. These were complemented by a single 0.50in gun mounted in each wing. On production aircraft, however, the engine-cowling guns were deleted and the wing armament increased to six 0.50in heavy machine-guns (three per wing), making the Corsair a very formidable gun platform. Later, 200 F4U-1C models were fitted with four 20mm Hispano cannon, though the heavy machine-gun arrangement proved more popular in service.

The most noticeable external alterations were focused on the cockpit area. First, the original wing-mounted fuel tanks were replaced by a much larger fuel tank directly behind the engine. This resulted in the cockpit being moved 32in rearwards to accommodate the larger fuel cell. This initiated a series of cockpit seating and canopy alterations that evolved with the aircraft. The cockpit canopy underwent three obvious visual changes during the aircraft's production run, and provides one of the easiest ways of distinguishing Corsair marks. The prototype and early F4U-1s had the 'birdcage'-type canopy, with multiple glazing bars securing the canopy glass in position. The F4U-1A, FG-1A and F3A-1 had an updated 'semi-blown' canopy with only two high-mounted glazing bars to improve visibility. All later marks had the full-blown type of canopy with no glazing bars, improving visibility still further.

On 2 April 1941 the US Navy placed a contract with the Vought Corporation for 584 Corsairs, designated F4U-1 (factory designation VS-317). The first production Corsair rolled off the assembly line on 25 June 1942.

On 21 September 1942 the first aircraft-carrier deck-landing trials of the Corsair took place on the USS *Sangamon*. Despite the Corsair's generally good performance, a list of observations by the test pilot resulted in the fighter being declared not yet fit for carrier operations, something US Navy officials did not want to hear. Poor pilot visibility, cramped and restrictive canopy design, an over-bouncy undercarriage and alarming slow-speed stalling characteristics revealed themselves when the Corsair was brought on to a carrier deck for the first time.

The US Marine Corps did use the Corsair in active combat roles at Guadalcanal, in the Pacific, in February 1943, with a high degree of success. However, in this case the aircraft was operated from land-based airstrips, not as a carrier-borne fighter.

Still with a feared and unforgiving reputation where carrier landings were concerned, the Corsair was finally tamed by the Royal Navy's Fleet Air Arm (FAA), whose pilots became the first to successfully take the Corsair to the flight deck in operational service.

Much of the initial Corsair deck-landing training for FAA pilots took place in the USA, causing quite a few raised eyebrows at various passing-out parades. One veteran attached to an early training group recalled that, at his qualifying parade, some US Navy pilots asked him what they were receiving their wings for.

A view of the final assembly line in the Vought factory. This picture is dated December 1942, and these early 'bird-cage'-canopy Corsairs are nearing completion. The highly efficient Vought production line was soon turning out several hundred of these aircraft each month. *(Vought Aircraft Industries)*

Above: With hook, wheels and flaps down, a long, curved, left-hand approach to the carrier deck, keeping the batsman in view until the very last second and following his every signal, was the FAA pilot's technique for successful Corsair deck landings. *(FAAM)*

Right: Possibly undergoing modifications or fitment trials, this incomplete US Navy-specification Corsair is being worked on away from the main Goodyear factory assembly line. Note the morale-boosting tally board on the factory wall. Monthly schedule target 115 aircraft – number produced, 102. *(Goodyear Tire & Rubber)*

FG-1 . . . the famous Corsair . . . built by Goodyear from Chance-Vought designs. This fast-climbing, single-seat fighter is in the "over 400 m.p.h." class of high altitude warplanes.

"I THOUGHT GOODYEAR MADE TIRES?"
They do, but they also build complete
Corsair fighters for the Navy and Marines.

POST CARD

GOODYEAR AIRCRAFT

Goodyear factory publicity
postcard from 1944.
(*Goodyear Tire & Rubber*)

'Deck-landing Corsairs' was his innocent answer.

'No, what have you really got them for?' was the quizzical response from an amused disbeliever.

A combination of further modifications by Vought, a revised landing procedure adopted by the FAA, which was familiar with difficult and often poorly adapted or modified aircraft for carrier use, and the determined efforts of both US and British airmen finally proved the Corsair to be a truly successful carrier-borne fighter.

Not surprisingly, Vought, as the parent design company, produced the greatest number of Corsairs (the overall total figure is quoted as 7,829), and at peak production was claiming an output of 300 aircraft a month. This is entirely believable, and compares with the wartime output of other American aircraft manufacturers. For example, Grumman Aircraft was at one stage producing so many Hellcat fighters (quoted at 600 per month at the peak rate) that the US government and Navy indicated that a slow-down in production might be necessary if ferry pilots were unable to ship them fast enough.

Although it was satisfied with the quality and output of aircraft from the Vought factory, the US Navy also co-contracted the Brewster Aeronautical Corporation of Long Island, New York, to build the Corsair, designated F3A-1, at its Johnsville, Pennsylvania, plant. Sadly the quality of the Brewster-built machines could not match that of the Vought product, and many of them were relegated to training use only. Brewster's production rate was also a major problem, being hindered by various factory management and worker scandals that contributed to the company's decline. Precise factory records and figures are difficult to obtain, but most sources state that a total of 732 Corsairs were delivered from Brewster. The FAA Museum's (FAAM) project would benefit greatly from more accurate information and listings concerning Brewster Corsair production, particularly in the final days of the factory's existence. Whatever the final total, only a small number of Corsairs were delivered before the US government intervened and finally brought about the complete closure of the Brewster Corporation on 30 June 1944.

Dozens of brand-new Goodyear-built Corsairs await their turn for a test flight at the Akron, Ohio, factory airfield. *(Goodyear Tire & Rubber)*

A more successful arrangement was contracted with the Goodyear Aircraft Company of Akron, Ohio, whose build quality and output was such that, by the end of production, nearly 4,000 Goodyear Corsairs (designated FG-1) had been constructed for full operational use. Depending on design modification dates, the designations FG-1A and FG-1D were assigned to Goodyear Corsairs. Because some aircraft were diverted from the production line for trials or redevelopment it is difficult to arrive at a definitive production total, but reliable sources in the Goodyear factory archive put it closer to 3,714.

With the longest production run of any American piston-engine fighter (1941–53), and its significant contribution to the air power available during the Second World War (and later in Korea, Indo-China and Suez), the Corsair has carved itself a worthy place in aviation history.

Three Goodyear-built Corsairs in close formation high over Akron, Ohio, in the summer of 1944. Goodyear test pilot Chris Clark, who made the first test flight of Corsair KD431, is flying the lead aircraft, 580. *(Goodyear Tire & Rubber)*

Chapter Two

Corsairs *in the* Fleet Air Arm

Without doubt, the Corsair was one of the most successful Second World War aircraft in terms of both design and achievement. Considering that its initial design was laid down in what was still essentially the biplane era, it was ahead of its time in many ways.

As a newly designed naval fighter the Corsair was specifically intended to be operated from the deck of an aircraft carrier. It is therefore no great surprise that it was soon offered for use by Britain's FAA under the wartime Lend-Lease arrangement between the British and US governments. As previously mentioned, the Corsair underwent many development changes, and for a while appeared to be inadequate for deck-landing operations. At some point in its development and trials programme it would surely have been developed into a successful deck-landing aircraft by the American or British Services. However, a combination of fate and timing, as much as skill and understanding of the intricacies of deck landing, gives the credit for this achievement to the FAA.

A system was set up whereby FAA pilots were sent to the USA to undergo a flying training programme that would culminate in their being qualified to fly the Corsair. Each batch of new recruits carried out classroom studies and also flying training on basic trainers such as the ever-popular Boeing Stearman and Ryan PT-25. Having completed this basic course, pilots progressed on to heavier types such as the Vultee Valiant or North American Harvard before finally graduating on to the Corsair. This training programme, which typically lasted some ten months, was spread among a number of airfields in various States, and provided many young British pilots with their first taste of life in a new country, and certainly their first introduction to the American way of life. If nothing else, it was a welcome change from the bleak, ration-governed way of life of wartime Britain, and most pilots interviewed by the author regarding this period of their career remember it with fondness.

Having completed their training and converted on to the Corsair, the young pilots faced the final hurdle of demonstrating their deck-landing abilities before finally receiving their 'wings', the official insignia worn on the uniform of all qualified pilots. In some cases, FAA pilots who qualified in the USA were awarded US Navy wings before they received their FAA

wings. This appears to have been generally approved by most pilots, as they could therefore end up with two different types of insignia.

Their training finally completed, each batch of newly qualified pilots was formed into a recognised squadron, to proceed with advanced flying training or perhaps going straight into active front-line service.

The first squadron to form with the Corsairs as its assigned aircraft was 1830 Naval Air Squadron (NAS). Having followed one of these familiar US training routes, 1830 NAS formed at Quonset Point, Maine, in the USA on 1 June 1943. Many others followed in quick succession, and by the war's end a large number of FAA squadrons had either newly formed or converted on to Corsairs by such a route. The number of FAA squadrons using Corsairs is frequently quoted as nineteen, but this refers only to front-line, active combat squadrons. No fewer than a further twenty second-line FAA squadrons used Corsairs for training, support and

A formation of Corsairs from HMS *Formidable* preparing to head for the strike on the German battleship *Tirpitz*. The aircraft launched about 90 miles from the Norwegian coast and covered a further 60 or so miles over bleak mountainous terrain to find their target tucked into an inlet of Kaa Fjord in northern Norway. *(FAAM)*

1835 Squadron Corsairs practise flight deck range parking on the 'airfield dummy deck' at HMS *Eglinton*, Northern Ireland, in June 1945. This exercise trained pilots and deck crews to park aircraft as tightly as possible (with engines running) on a ship's flight deck, but allowing each aircraft to be able to taxi forward in turn for take-off. *(FAAM)*

auxiliary duties, bringing the true total of FAA squadrons that used Corsairs at some point during their histories to forty.

The early squadrons used a mixture of Vought F4U-1, F4U-1A and 1D types, known to the British as the Mks I and II respectively, and the Brewster-built F3A-1s, known to the British as the Mk III. Later squadrons were equipped with Goodyear-built FG-1A and FG-1D Corsairs, both referred to as the Mk IV by the British.

The first hostile action for FAA Corsairs occurred on 3 April 1944. Corsairs of 1834 NAS (HMS *Victorious*) joined forces with Grumman Hellcats of 800 NAS (HMS *Emperor*), Grumman Wildcats of 898 NAS (HMS *Searcher*) and Supermarine Seafires of 801 NAS (HMS *Furious*) to provide fighter cover for Fairey Barracudas executing dive-bombing attacks on the German battleship *Tirpitz* in a Norwegian fjord. The attack was a resounding success. During July and August of that year Corsairs of 1841 and 1842 NAS provided fighter cover for further strikes against German shipping in Norwegian waters.

April 1944 also saw the first FAA Corsair action with the East Indies Fleet, Corsairs from 1830 and 1833 NAS (HMS *Illustrious*) providing fighter cover and fleet-defence patrols during raids on Sabang. Many significant and historic battles in the Eastern and Pacific war theatres owe much to the robust, powerful and potent Corsair fighter-bomber.

Indeed, the second of two Victoria Cross gallantry awards made to the FAA during the Second World War was to a Corsair pilot. On 9 August 1945 Lt R.H. Gray, a Royal Canadian Volunteer Reserve pilot flying with the FAA, led an attack that earned him the award but sadly cost him his life. Gray led a formation of Corsairs of 1841 NAS (HMS *Formidable*) on a daring low-level attack against Japanese shipping in the Tokyo area. He pressed home the attack against extremely intense and accurate enemy fire from both ground installations and ships. The squadron inflicted a significant amount of damage to the area, and Lt Gray scored a direct hit on a Japanese destroyer with a single bomb from his Corsair, causing the vessel to sink in the harbour. Tragically, moments later, Gray's Corsair was

Engineers and armourers from 1833 Squadron HMS *Illustrious* make ready a Corsair with 500lb bombs. The 'D' type Corsair bomb mounting arrangement on the underside of the inner wing stub can be seen clearly. Note the lack of safety shoes and equipment required by deck crews in 1944. *(FAAM)*

Airfitters and engineers from 1843 Squadron HMS *Arbiter* find a corner of the flight deck to remove the engine from a Corsair. The date is not known, however the white shorts would indicate an Eastern or Pacific theatre of war. The aircraft appears to have suffered some front-end damage, possibly a barrier collision, but is apparently not beyond repair. *(FAAM)*

seen to crash into the sea. He was posthumously awarded the Victoria Cross for his bravery and devotion to duty in leading this successful attack.

At the time of the Japanese surrender there were eight FAA Corsair squadrons operational in the Pacific theatre. However, with the war against Japan at an end, many Corsair squadrons were swiftly disbanded, only four front-line Corsair squadrons, 1831, 1846, 1850 and 1851 NAS, remaining by the latter part of 1945. Several second-line units continued to use the Corsair into 1946. The date of the last flight by an FAA Corsair is currently unknown, but it was probably made by one of the Corsairs operated by 721 NAS at Kai Tak airfield, Hong Kong, during 1947. By the end of this period some 1,977 Corsairs had been delivered to Great Britain, but, remarkably, by the mid-1950s only KD431 survived as a complete example of an FAA Corsair.

Chapter Three

Flight *from* Ceylon

What of the story of the aircraft that flew back from Ceylon? Did it actually happen, and, if so, who did it? Could it be substantiated, and what was the identity of the aircraft involved? All of these questions lay behind the research to find out if this was really how KD431 became a postwar survivor. This research would also provide the foundation of what we knew about the finish, originality and condition of KD431, and determine how we would proceed with further investigations.

The pilot who made the alleged flight was Lt Cdr Godfrey Woodbine-Parish DSC, affectionately known to his close friends and colleagues as GWP, or 'God', a former FAA fighter pilot who visited the Fleet Air Arm Museum (FAAM) in the early 1970s and claimed that KD431 was the aircraft he had used for this journey. Unfortunately he was unable to locate his flying log book, and he died in 1974, leaving no accurate written account of the flight. A few close friends and family members recall various snippets of detail regarding the event, but conclusive proof that KD431 was the aircraft involved has never been found. Hopefully, the author has now pieced together sufficient information to make some sense of this legend.

Lt Cdr Godfrey Woodbine-Parish, DSC. *(E. Horsford)*

THE MAN HIMSELF

Born in 1919, Godfrey Woodbine-Parish, DSC, had by the age of 24 attained the rank of acting lieutenant commander in the FAA, possibly being one of the youngest to receive such a commission at that time. He was awarded the DSC in 1942 for action during Operation *Harpoon*, the official citation in the *London Gazette* reading: 'Awarded the DSC for bravery and resolution in HM ship EAGLE while escorting an important convoy to Malta.'

Generally well liked and a talented aviator (by 1944 he was the commanding officer of 757 Sqn, Fighter Training School, Puttalam, Ceylon), GWP was also renowned for his self-will, determination and no-nonsense approach to life.

Commander Lionel Hooke and CPO Hubert Hartley were both attached to 757 Sqn at the time GWP was its CO, and have their own fond recollections of this extraordinary man. Hartley was an air fitter attached to 757 Sqn at Puttalam. He recalls:

> GWP, one day, had reached the end of his tether at the amount of pilots taxying their aircraft off the edge of the airfield perimeter track that made a winding route through the palm trees of this jungle airfield. Often, such an error of judgement would require the use of an elephant (towing tractors were in short supply) to pull the stricken aircraft back on to the perimeter track. This was obviously time-consuming and could often result in unnecessary damage to the aircraft.

An item not normally found on a squadron ground equipment register. Fifi the elephant, sporting her own naval uniform cap, carefully manoeuvres a 757 Sqn Corsair at Puttalam in 1944. *(U. Bagnall)*

In a bid to emphasise to the pilots that this simple ground manoeuvre should not be so problematic, he took off in a Fairey Fulmar aircraft and followed the winding perimeter track course at low level, with the wings of his aircraft at times nearly vertical, so as to thread his way through the tree-lined track route. Hubert Hartley continues:

It was an amazing piece of flying – I stood in the middle of the airfield and watched him take off and fly the Fulmar around the perimeter track, at times no higher than the tops of the palm trees, to show the other pilots that it could be done flying, let alone taxying on the ground – I would not have believed it if I had not seen it for myself.

When asked if he recalled GWP flying back to England in a Corsair, he could not remember such an event, but added: 'I should not be surprised; it was typical of God – if anyone would have done it, he would have.'

Cdr Hooke was at that time a sub-lieutenant pilot attached to 757 Sqn at Puttalam (at the time in 1943 when GWP was the squadron commanding officer in charge of fighter training and deck landing). While there he received a draft instruction to operate with the Army in Burma, returning again to Ceylon while on passage home. The following extracts are key points from conversations with Cdr Hooke regarding this period, and what he recalls of the GWP legend.

Some mysteries surround GWP. I last saw him when I left the squadron [757 Puttalam] at the end of our tour. I was posted for a short time with the Army in Burma, returning to Ceylon whilst en route back home.

It was then that I heard that 'God' had set off for home in a Seafire aircraft, getting as far as Bombay before a serviceability problem with the aircraft halted his progress. Being immediately returned to Puttalam, he apparently set out again at the next possible opportunity in a Corsair aircraft.

When I was offered the alternative of a sea trip home in the next convoy or a flight (when available), my former Ceylon colleagues suggested that 'I do a Godfrey' – i.e. take an aircraft and fly myself.

I chose a ship as I knew my brother-in-law was chief engineer on the heavy lift ship in the same convoy, which I felt may be advantageous, and a cruise in a 'luxury liner' was preferable before the rigours of Whale Island and a SNAW [School of Naval Air Warfare] course. Anyway, I had just done a 4,500-miler by air and remembered it all too well. I also did not have Godfrey's muscle in appropriation of aircraft.

There was a dearth of homeward-bound ships and planes at the time, and I gather he decided to fly himself back as the route by then was well defined. It was possible to hitch a lift home, as at that time we flew willy-nilly all over India, either in our own aircraft, the Navy's [Beech] Expeditors or RAF DC-3s [Douglas Dakotas]. Certainly by January 1945 one could fly home officially or by hitching a lift from either Bombay or Calcutta if you were required home urgently.

As the squadron CO he had the right to authorise such journeys, and things like that happened all the time when ashore in the mystic East.

When you are master of your own destiny, any signal which read 'By air if possible', means if you are keen, you do just that – grab the nearest aeroplane and go!

I personally only discovered this freewheeling facility when sent on my own further East.

It was my belief that 'God' had suffered mildly from Malaria, and it was a concern (at the time) that his eyesight may in time become affected.

He was, however, one of the best COs for 757 to meet the demands of the 'new' Pacific Fleet training. Therefore, his return to the UK for leave, medicals and reappointment to a training squadron was inevitable, and justified his urgent return to the UK.

Interesting though they are, these recollections still offer no conclusive proof that GWP made the flight back to England, or used KD431 to do so.

Godfrey Woodbine-Parish's own recollection of the journey, and the reference to 'doing a Godfrey' by some personnel stationed at Puttalam certainly suggest that some extraordinary event took place, but how could this be proved?

Given the lack of flying log books or a personal diary that might have answered that question, it was hoped that the answer might be found in the official Royal Naval Archives. Regardless of rank or posting, every serving member of the Royal Navy or FAA was required to provide notification of their arrival at, or departure from, any military base as a matter of procedure. There were security implications, and it was necessary to keep track of any food and pay requirements. If GWP had journeyed from Ceylon to England in a military aircraft he would have had to make stops for rest and refuelling. Most, if not all, of these stops would have been at military air bases capable of refuelling and/or repairing his aircraft without too many questions being asked. However, we are led to believe that this was an unofficial flight, and may not have been recorded as thoroughly as would normally be required.

A study of information concerning the period 1 January 1945 to March 1946, the dates between which GWP is believed to have made the flight, provided a basis for some logical deductions. Limited information, pieced together from a variety of sources, reveals the following:

On 1 January 1945 Godfrey Woodbine-Parish was serving at HMS *Rajaliyah* (RN base) Puttalam, Ceylon. On 23 August 1945 he took passage home (method of passage not recorded), arriving first at HMS *St Angelo* (RN base), Malta, on 9 September 1945, some seventeen days later. His passage appears to have recommenced three days later, on 12 September 1945, and he arrived at HMS *Daedalus* (RN base) Lee-on-Solent, Hampshire, England, on 21 September 1945.

The total journey time appears to be about twenty-nine days, though any method of transport or passage has yet to be ascertained. Had GWP flown an extended route, making unauthorised stops at both military and non-military bases, the journey might well have spanned one month. However, ship travelling time between the two destinations falls into a similar time span.

By this time in 1945 the Suez Canal was open to shipping, so a fifteen-to twenty-day journey time between Ceylon and Malta would be entirely possible. However, a flight route from Ceylon, with stops perhaps at Cochin, Coimbatore, Bombay, Karachi; then Muscat, Dubai or Oman; then Baghdad, Amman and Cairo (his sister Elizabeth remembers him bringing scent and silk goods from Cairo and Bombay, indicating that enough time was taken to explore the local markets); then Alexandria, Mersa Matruh and Al Bayda or Benghazi, before crossing to Malta, would have also taken around twenty days, making allowance for weather, refuelling, flight clearance, overnight stops and the like.

The remainder of the journey, from Malta to Great Britain in nine days, is again a similarly plausible time scale, either by ship or in short-stage flights in a single-engine aircraft. We cannot, therefore, determine how GWP made the journey by comparing travelling times alone. However, he was alleged to have procured some French brandy somewhere en route, which could indicate a trans-Europe leg.

Such a flight in a single-engine aircraft would have been gruelling in the extreme, testing both man and machine to the limit. The distances between some of these more obvious, potential (and surmised) staging points would be approaching the maximum range for a Corsair, even with long-range fuel tanks.

Each location would also have to have a suitable landing field and the provision of fuel as a bare minimum, and any unserviceability or break-down, with no suitable spares back-up, would have left pilot and aircraft high and dry. Moreover, some of the legs would have entailed crossing dangerously wide stretches of desert and sea.

If the flight was made over a route similar to the one outlined above, the risk would have been vast and the capability of the pilot exceptional. However, such capabilities and qualities had been shown by Godfrey Woodbine-Parish, as evidenced in numerous FAA documents and reports throughout his naval career.

One interesting question is why the final destination for his return passage on 21 September 1945 is listed as HMS *Daedalus* (Lee-on-Solent). This was an FAA airfield, rather than a seaport, which leads one to ask whether GWP flew in to this destination or arrived at Portsmouth by sea and passed through HMS *Daedalus* to collect instructions for his next posting.

What we do now know is that GWP left Ceylon in August 1945 and arrived back in England in September 1945. We can also now be sure (albeit sadly) that the journey was not made in KD431. Conclusive proof in at least two separate pilots' log books show that KD431 was attached to 1835 Sqn in England in July 1945, and handed over to 768 Sqn in September 1945.

Trawling through the hundreds of serial numbers of FAA Corsairs did yield further possibilities (or confusions), but no conclusive evidence.

One listing has a Corsair with the serial KD341 attached to 757 Sqn at Puttalam at this time. However, records appear to show (assuming they are accurate) that this aircraft was officially struck off charge in Trincomalee on 1 January 1946, having suffered a minor accident at Puttalam in July 1945.

Other confusable identities or possible number transpositions are as follows:

JT431 1837 Sqn: July 1944 tested at RNAY Coimbatore, India; 9 September 1944 moved to 1834 Sqn and suffered a deck-landing accident on HMS *Victorious*, 15 September 1944. The final whereabouts of this similarly numbered aircraft is unknown.

JT341 1837 Sqn: attached to this squadron at this time, but final whereabouts unknown, 25 July 1944.

KD413 1831 Sqn: flown from Pityilu to RNAS Ponam Manus Islands, but final whereabouts unknown, 12 September 1945.

Available research material and records have grown vastly since the first text and brief diary relating to KD431 was compiled and displayed at the FAAM in the early 1970s and, regrettably, some of this earlier information has proved incorrect. The full up-to-date diary of KD431 appears in Appendix II on page 194. One must also consider that other records concerning the final whereabouts of similarly numbered and confusable aircraft may or may not also contain errors, which could have a significant bearing on the whole story.

The manner in which Woodbine-Parish returned from Ceylon is still not fully understood, and, until conclusive evidence surfaces, mystery continues to surround this epic adventure.

Chapter Four

The **Great Challenge**

If KD431 did not make a round trip to Ceylon and back, what did it do during its short career with the FAA and in the remaining years before it became a museum exhibit? To understand this fully it was necessary to remove the most recent paint layer, applied in 1963 when the aircraft arrived at the FAAM, and map this against an extremely in-depth research study of the aircraft.

This thorough and painstaking approach eventually yielded a complete record of what had happened to the aircraft during its manufacture, Service life and its time on display in the museum. In essence, it provided as full and completely researched an understanding of an aircraft as can be achieved.

Corsair KD431 on display before restoration work began in 2000. Although it looks neat and tidy, many markings and colours have been incorrectly positioned and inaccurately applied. Could what lay beneath be rediscovered, and what might it reveal about the aircraft's true history? Note the modern jet-aircraft tyres fitted in this picture. *(FAAM)*

All too often one hears the generalised summing-up of procedures or techniques performed in factory production or Service life expressed as 'we always did this', or 'it was always done like that', or, even worse, 'I'm sure they would have done this'. Such sweeping statements offer little historical accuracy and are often only opinions or, at best, fading recollections.

As I have never been involved in factory production or military service, it might be argued that my knowledge of the object aircraft and its background would be lacking and insufficient to attempt such a task. However, the fact that I had few or no preconceived ideas about how work may have been performed allowed me to view the evidence with fresh eyes and thoughts, and to ask questions. This ensured that everything was examined with the sole intention of observing, theorising, deducing and arriving, where possible, at a conclusion based purely on the

Corsair KD431 at Cranfield College, 1963. Photographs such as this were used in the restorer's research to plot and map original features such as wing markings, squadron codes and wheel and tyre details before restoration work started. (J. Fricker FRAeS)

evidence before me. The disproving of a few popular myths or theories inevitably sat uncomfortably in some circles, but in part this was what the exercise was all about; being dissatisfied with what might have happened, and trying to prove what actually did happen.

There was also the hope that this project would encourage thoughts on how to deal with twentieth-century mechanical objects in general. If the results of this exercise helped to change the way people dealt with the historical mechanical objects or vehicles in their care, then hopefully some wider historical good would result.

Why do people feel such a need to tamper with a vehicle's originality, yet immediately see the error of performing a similar act on a piece of fine art or furniture? 'Restored to its original condition' or 'former glory' are terms frequently applied to the stripping, repainting and presentation of artefacts. Surely they should be described as 'refinished', 'rebuilt', or

perhaps even 'defaced to non-original condition'? Scratches, marks and the patina that is so readily recognised as proof of originality and value on domestic antiques suddenly become intolerable in the quest to produce a gleaming, flawless object when the subject is a machine. Some objects might have deteriorated so completely that full refurbishment is the best route to take, and owners have the right to treat their objects as they choose. Who, though, will have the truly original examples when all of the others have been irreversibly defaced to non-original condition?

TESTING THE THEORY

Before any paint removal began on KD431, a very thorough photograph research exercise was carried out. As many images as possible depicting the aircraft between 1944 and 1999 were amassed. These were used to create a time-line of images to indicate where changes to the colours, markings and details of the aircraft had occurred during that period. This was vital to provide an accurate working reference, even though it was mostly in black and white. Many weeks were spent analysing and making notes from these images to enable key details to be looked for as work progressed.

Starting at the beginning, or in this case with the nose of the aircraft, made sense, but a little more thought and logic was applied at the start of this project. Knowing what one wanted to achieve was vital at this point. What I hoped could be achieved was the uncovering or revealing of an aircraft in its original paintwork as applied at factory-build stage, and bearing the witness marks and modifications of its short Service career. Much of the work would be experimental, building on techniques discovered and practised on previous projects.

Taking the propeller-hub cover as a starting point meant that the experiment was firstly defined within the cover itself, a small component approximately 9in long by 6in in diameter, and domed at one end. Any error at this stage would not risk a large area of the aircraft's surface finish. Research had already indicated that the finish on this component did not appear to be original (many references will be made to the Cranfield photograph of *c.* 1956). On Service aircraft the colours of the propeller hub and spinner cover were often changed in accordance with squadron and unit markings, so the likelihood of this area already having been tampered with or defaced was high.

Even the seemingly most obvious areas need to be constantly checked against available research material to ensure that the thought process, evaluation of findings (which keeps changing) and techniques can be reviewed, altered and kept in line with each other. I cannot emphasise strongly enough that stop-and-think time is the most valuable time of all.

The small bolt that holds the propeller hub cover in position represents the forward-most part of the aircraft. This was the starting point for examination and work leading to a systematic, section-by-section study of the entire aircraft.

Limited at this stage by black-and-white reference photographs, all thoughts, theories and findings had to be very carefully considered to determine what was original or deemed to date from, or fit within, the time-span of August 1944 (the date the aircraft was completed) to May 1946 (the date it was decommissioned from service). The aim was to restore the aircraft to appear just as it did in this period.

The Cranfield photograph clearly shows this bolt head, and the hub cover itself, to be in a uniform dark finish, unlike the bright yellow brush-painted finish that was now applied to the head of the bolt. This finish appeared to date from the enhancing touch-up work applied to the aircraft shortly after its arrival at Yeovilton in 1963. Comparison with photographs seemed to confirm this.

The yellow paint had not adhered particularly well to the bolt head. It could easily be picked away using a scalpel blade, revealing a good-quality black paint finish beneath. This had been applied over a green/yellow chromate primer that gave every indication of being the factory-applied finish. Careful removal of the bolt revealed that the black paint continued on the underside of the washer (seated between the bolt and the hub cover) and on the crown of the dome beneath the washer. This suggested that both components had later been refinished in their respective yellow and red while fitted to the aircraft, and that these colours were not factory-applied.

Can we do it? Yes we can. The red-painted propeller-hub cover is returned to its original factory-applied black paint finish. The small area of paint missing from the red hub represents the very first flake of paint removed at the start of the project. *(FAAM)*

The hub cover itself had been spray painted with a bright red gloss paint, probably an oil-based enamel. It appeared to have been applied at the same time and in the same manner as the red circles around the wing gun port-holes. Again research showed that this red finish was apparently applied shortly after the aircraft's arrival at Yeovilton in 1963. This paint finish was also found to be lifting, and could be carefully picked away using a small knife blade and a plastic scraper, again revealing a black paint finish beneath.

Thankfully the red paint had been applied directly on to the black finish, apparently with no primer, undercoat or abrading of the surface. This enabled the red finish again to be removed relatively easily to reveal what remained of the black beneath. Was this the original finish applied to these propeller components in 1944? It is easy to jump to the conclusion that it was, but it would be some months before a colour photograph became available to help verify this and many other findings.

Corsair KD431 in the FAAM restoration hangar in January 2000. A lot of work lay ahead, and many interesting details were to emerge during the restoration. *(N. Pratlett)*

Despite careful working, some black paint was removed with the red finish. This problem was reviewed at several stages, and considered acceptable if the loss could be kept to a minimum. A study of various Cranfield photographs clearly showed that some areas of this paint were already missing by the time the aircraft left the college.

Removing paint is hardly a new skill or science, but the proof that it was possible to remove the 1963 paint layers and leave enough of the original 1944 factory finish intact offered an exciting new possibility. Could we remove all of the recently applied paint and reveal a 'time-capsule' aircraft of sixty years ago? It had been done often enough with fine art or furniture; why not with an entire aircraft?

It had to be tried, in a careful and measured way so as not to risk the aircraft as an historical museum object, and studied and recorded stage by stage to create a documentary record of the aircraft.

ONE CHANCE TO GET IT RIGHT

A few square inches are one thing, but a whole aircraft is a different matter. This seemingly impossible task was further complicated by the need to be looking constantly at the whole aircraft to spot clues, understand what had happened, and use this as a basis for thought and theory processes. Coupled with this was the need to focus on each small defined work section so as not to miss a vital clue or piece of historic evidence and maintain accuracy, without becoming demoralised by the size of the task.

In addition, there was the awareness that the object that was to be 'set about' with abrasives, scrapers and the like was probably the last known complete surviving original example. If we messed it up there would be no second chance; at least, not with a Corsair.

Chapter Five

Step *by* Step
and What Was Found

Aircraft can easily be divided into areas of work that can be managed, contained or defined by individual components or by skin and rivet lines, for example. This made the systematic approach we adopted very much easier to control, understand and record.

What follows is a section-by-section, nose-to-tail examination of the aircraft, listing the findings (and theories) along the way. The level of detail might seem excessive, but the manner in which these aircraft were actually treated and produced at factory level, and the alterations carried out in Service, are fast being forgotten or, at best, only vaguely recalled by the few survivors of those involved at the time. How often have we wished that we could be transported back in time to ask questions or witness events? How often do we wish that an object could talk to us? Here, on the brink of a lost age, was the chance to study an historical object and discuss and compile the evidence with the few surviving witnesses. The importance of this study might not be fully appreciated for many years to come.

With only a few reference photographs to work from could we really take KD431 back in time? *(FAAM)*

PROPELLER HUB AND PROPELLER BLADES

On examination, the propeller hub was found to be coated in a very lightly applied matt black emulsion paint. This had been applied on top of a much harder black finish (though this had been eroded or flaked away in some areas). Study of the Cranfield photograph does indeed show a dark (possibly black) finish on the hub, but which of the two was original?

Emulsion would not normally be applied to such a component on Service aircraft. Furthermore, there appeared to be faint traces of black overspray on the front outer lips of the engine cowlings immediately behind the propeller, suggesting recent respray work. Turning the propeller itself soon revealed that these overspray marks aligned perfectly with the three propeller blades and corresponding hub fittings. The conclusion at this stage was that the hub had been relatively recently resprayed with the emulsion finish.

Looking now at the blades themselves, we found that they had also been sprayed over with a similar soft black finish (probably the same emulsion). This was a poorly executed job, with no attempt to mask off the original

Another key reference photograph showing KD431 at Cranfield in 1956. Propeller damage can be seen in this picture, and also the painted-on engine inhibiting reference date, though the latter is not clear enough to be fully readable. *(Cranfield University Archive)*

31

manufacturer's transfers. This finish adhered to the blade as poorly as it did to the hub, and very light application of a fine plastic scraper removed it easily. Beneath was a much more substantial satin black finish, looking clearly more akin to the type of finish applied to the blades at factory level. Working carefully along the leading edge of one of the blades revealed erosion marks typical of those found on propeller blades in service. Comparison with the 1956 Cranfield photograph soon revealed that many of the erosion marks matched, confirming that the blade in question was the same as that fitted in the Cranfield photograph, and that the soft black finish had been applied after this photograph was taken.

The Cranfield photograph also showed that one blade had suffered more severe erosion, perhaps even damage. Further examination revealed that this blade was still fitted to the aircraft, the damaged area having been concealed by a layer of cellulose body filler and overpainted black. Enough witness marks were now evident to confirm that the propeller set fitted to the aircraft was the same as in the Cranfield photograph.

The soft black finish appears to have been a repair and enhancement job carried out shortly after the Corsair's arrival at Yeovilton. Carefully, this paint finish was completely removed to reveal the original factory finish beneath. In some areas on the blade roots there were traces of red overspray, implying that, when the red finish had been applied to the hub cover, the component had been poorly masked.

Careful attention was taken around the transfers and an area of a blade that showed white hand-painted wording, roughly applied, that appeared (in the Cranfield photograph) to read: 'don't turn engine [date unreadable]'. Such a marking is typical of that applied to all aircraft that have had their engines inhibited and been relegated to storage, as turning the propeller and hence the engine would mar the inhibiting process. Small traces of this white paint still existed, and have been left intact on the blade, but insufficient remained to enable the date to be deciphered.

This engine inhibiting process could really only have happened in one of two places. One was the Cranfield College of Aeronautics, where the aircraft went in 1946, but this was unlikely, as the aircraft would have been viewed as a workshop demonstration object rather than an aircraft to be preserved for further or future use. The other was Donibristle, where the aircraft was sent for storage immediately after its Service life, to await disposal or further use.

This seemingly insignificant fact plays quite an important part in understanding KD431's history. The exact date when this aircraft left naval service is currently unknown, and if the date on the propeller

A close-up of the damaged propeller blade. The score marks and scars had been hidden beneath black paint and cellulose filler in 1963, but what was their origin? The small patch of white paint at the centre of the propeller blade is all that remains of the hand-painted reference to when the engine was inhibited for storage. *(FAAM)*

Date	Unit	Locus	Aircraft		Docket	CATEGORY		
			Type		No.	Cause		Code
27.9.45	768.	Ballyhalbert	Corsair. KD431			1st deck landing / a/c floated up deck, catching No. 8 wire & entering barrier		

SURNAME. Foulkes. CHRISTIAN NAME. J.Dp.
RANK. S/Lt. (A). RNVR. NUMBER.

ACCIDENTS

blade could be deciphered it would provide a more accurate picture of its movements at the time.

Careful cleaning around the transfers applied to the blades has enabled these original Hamilton Standard Company items to be preserved. However, one blade seems to have been refinished in the correct manufacturer's black finish over the top of its transfer. It is not known whether this blade was replaced during its service in the FAA, or refinished in this way at the factory.

With all propeller blades now cleaned of their emulsion paint and filler, a thorough examination of the damaged areas was possible. The main damage, as seen in the photograph, consisted of a series of evenly spaced scores in the blade surfaces. This damage was very deep on the front face of one blade, and similar but less deep or extensive on the rear face of another. The heavily scarred area showed signs of having been dressed smooth to effect a repair. But how did this damage occur? Was it the result of a ground-handling or road transportation accident during one of the aircraft's many movements around Great Britain, or was it the result of an in-service incident?

An accident record (A25 report form) dating from 27 September 1945 still existed, showing that the aircraft had indeed been involved in a deck-landing accident at this time. The entry reads: '1st deck landing – a/c floated up deck catching No. 8 wire & entering barrier.' This describes the all-too-familiar scenario of an aircraft landing on an aircraft carrier and catching the last arrester wire spanning the deck while still travelling forward in semi-flight, without having come properly to rest. In such an instance a barrier screen of large steel wires would be raised immediately ahead of the aircraft to prevent it from colliding with aircraft parked further forward on the deck.

Details of aircraft accidents were normally recorded on the official form A25. Digging deep into the FAAM archive resulted in the original A25 card being produced which referred to the incident that caused the propeller damage to KD431. This lucky find provided both the date and the pilot's name.
(Crown Copyright/MoD)

Looking again at the blades, and considering the rotation of the propeller, it seemed likely that the damage could have been caused by a heavy steel cable being dragged across the front face of one blade that was rotating at speed and travelling forwards at the same time, the cable then being caught behind the following blade as the aircraft ground to a halt.

A further study of squadron records (the aircraft was in the hands of 768 Sqn at this time) showed that the aircraft was being operated successfully in November 1945. The fact that the aircraft was operational again within such a short space of time clearly indicated that the deck-landing incident was unlikely to have caused severe damage. Although this is a sound theory, it is not conclusively proven as yet. It would help if we could speak to the pilot responsible, but what chance is there of that?

ENGINE

Following in sequence behind the propeller is the engine itself. The Pratt & Whitney Double Wasp, an impressive 18-cylinder two-row radial engine, was capable of producing over 2,000hp. Very few aircraft manufacturers produce their own engines, opting instead to fit a unit successfully designed, developed and produced by an engine manufacturer in its own right, in this case the Pratt & Whitney company of East Hartford, Connecticut, USA. Most of the engine inspection and data plates were in place, but we immediately encountered another problem that needed solving. The actual manufacturer's plate had sadly been lost from the front engine casing, having either been removed for some logical reason or stolen. Not only was this intensely annoying, but it also made it impossible to determine whether the engine was made by Pratt & Whitney or was one of the units built under subcontract by the Ford Motor Company. It was common practice, particularly in wartime, to subcontract components and assemblies to other manufacturers with suitable production facilities. The motor industry in particular was an obvious choice, given its knowledge of high-quality mass-production techniques. Indeed, the Ford Motor Company of Great Britain undertook such contract work, producing Rolls-Royce Merlin engines as part of the war effort. However, without this particular plate it may be difficult to tell exactly where KD431's engine was manufactured.

The engine itself was in very good, complete, condition and appeared to retain its original factory finishes. Internally, viewed only through removed sparking-plug apertures, the engine was again in excellent condition, showing few or no signs of excessive wear. There was evidence that anti-corrosion and inhibiting solutions had been applied to most of the exterior (a soft semi-set oily wax, reddish brown in colour). Careful turning of

Opposite: This dramatic photograph shows a Corsair being brought to a halt by the ship's steel-wire safety barrier. A slow-speed collision with the barrier would result in only light damage to the aircraft, but a high-speed encounter such as this could be fatal for the pilot, and would almost certainly result in the aircraft being written off. The barrier height setting was also critical for safe recovery of different aircraft types. (This Corsair has East Indies Fleet roundels on its starboard wing and fuselage, and British Pacific Fleet insignia on its port wing.) *(FAAM)*

The mighty Pratt & Whitney R-2800 Double Wasp radial engine was squeezed beneath the cowlings with fractions of an inch to spare. *(FAAM)*

A close-up of the manufacturer's engine-installation ticket. The lack of damage or witness marks on this vulnerable paper ticket suggested that the engine had not been removed from the aircraft since it was installed in the factory. *(FAAM)*

the propeller also showed that the engine was not seized or locked in any way.

With the exception of the main fuel drain, all control linkages, pipes, connections, and so on, were still fully and properly connected, and the correct wire-locking and tag-sealing of ancillaries strongly indicated that the engine had not been dismantled since it was last in service, or since it left the factory. This was why internal inspection was limited to viewing through the spark-plug apertures, using an optical probe-scope device. Removal of any covers or components to gain access to the engine's internal components would have immediately and irreversibly destroyed the engine's 'time-capsule' originality. There can be few, if any, remaining examples of an engine fitted to an aircraft having such original features.

Even the way that components were wire-locked, sealed or tagged into place are part of the aircraft's history. If left intact and undisturbed they will serve as actual and accurate references to the engineering techniques and disciplines of the era. This may again seem extreme, but does it differ from wondering how a certain peg was installed or located in, say, a Viking ship hundreds of years ago, when no complete, original, unaltered examples survive?

Moving to the lower part of the engine bay and examining the mounting frame bolts revealed further interesting evidence. The lower left-hand mounting bolt is a recessed fitting. Still affixed to the wall of this recess is a pink-paper ticket bearing the legend 'power plant – A' (there appears to have been other printed lettering on the ticket, but this is now unreadable). From my own engineering experience, it is difficult to imagine fitting a large box or socket-type spanner into this tight recess and not tearing, dislodging or soiling this fragile paper ticket in some way. It is remarkable that it has survived, and its very existence is noteworthy. The bolt head itself bears no witness marks of having been removed and refitted, as often found on such components. Until build numbers become available it cannot be proved, but all the evidence points to this engine not having been removed from the aircraft since the day it was fitted at the factory.

The exhaust pipe open ends have traces of red oxide dope splashes, suggesting that the exhausts were blanked off at some stage after the engine was last run (engine running temperatures would burn away all such traces of paint or dope finishes). This would be typical practice for an aircraft having its engine inhibited and being laid up in storage. It is very likely that this work would have been carried out when KD431 left its last squadron, or while it was in storage at RNAY Donibristle. It is less likely to have been done at Cranfield, and almost certainly not since its arrival at Yeovilton. This could be clarified if it were possible to read the date painted on the propeller in the 1956 Cranfield reference photograph.

ENGINE COWLINGS AND COVERS

A BREAKTHROUGH

Removal of the forward engine cowlings was necessary to enable a full inspection of all areas of the engine. This, however, signalled the beginning of a far more interesting process than I could ever have imagined. Many coincidences and discoveries, the saving of many unique original features, plus meetings with many people with fascinating stories to tell, would knit together, resulting in a project that would challenge a few text and history books and result in a worthwhile conservation exercise.

The front engine cowl ring bolts directly to the engine cylinder heads. The brackets and fixings on this component certainly gave the impression that they had not been disturbed since being fitted at the factory. Little would be gained from the removal of the ring and, since the essence of this project was to preserve originality at all costs, it was left undisturbed. However, the dark grey/blue paintwork on this ring seemed to vary in colour and quality of finish over its surface. Light rubbing with metal polish wadding in a few selected areas soon revealed a much stronger and more uniform blue finish beneath. Some areas of the paint finish seemed to be more heavily applied or better adhered, so softening and removal by light rubbing with acrylic thinners, carefully applied, was employed. These two techniques, or a combination of the two, formed the basis of paint removal for most of the fuselage and wings.

(An accurate colour reference for the glossy sea blue colour had been found close to the aircraft's cockpit. A small area of fuselage immediately behind the cockpit was shielded by the rear flange of the cockpit canopy in both the open and closed positions, and had not been painted in 1963. It was also shielded from direct sunlight, and was therefore a good indicator of the colour blue that we needed to clean back to on the cowling ring and other areas of fuselage.)

A detail view showing the unusual factory-applied matt-white finish on the inside of the engine cowling. Most reference sources state that this area was finished in yellow chromate primer, or in the colour of the main fuselage paint scheme. (FAAM)

A close-up of one of the factory-applied stencils on a forward fuselage panel. With great care it proved possible to save these delicate original stencils during the paint removal process. (FAAM)

Interestingly, the inner surface of the engine cowling was finished in a light grey paint finish. All references to date show that, in this area, Corsairs were finished in either yellow chromate primer (like the rest of the airframe internals) or in the same colour finish as the outer surface of the cowling, which in this case would have been dark blue. Why light grey was used on this aircraft is unknown. The finish is original, as applied at the factory. It might have been a result of paint shortages or inconsistencies under wartime conditions, or it could have been an experiment, a mistake or perhaps what was specified for FAA aircraft. No official documentation appears to exist to explain this, and no other FAA Corsairs are known to remain to provide a comparison.

Close study under a magnifying glass of many photographs of Corsairs in service was vital to guide the team with regard to the position of markings, original factory stencilling, and other delicate features that needed to be preserved. (We also discovered that many small details or stencillings did not show up on photographs, making constant vigilance essential when working.) The first breakthrough came during early work on this cowling ring, with the discovery of original factory stencilling showing the locating position for a service platform. The paintwork around (and over the top of) the pale grey stencil block of lettering could be cleaned off sufficiently to enable the instruction to be read clearly against the original factory-applied glossy sea blue paint. There was still a long way to go, but again we felt a sense of real achievement. We had done it. We had returned to 1944; not replicated, copied or repainted, but restored to the actual original factory finish.

The art lies in knowing how far one dares to go with the thinners/wadding/abrasive process. Not far enough and the result is limited; a few seconds and a few rubs too many and your history is gone, a bleary stain on your rag, completely irreversible. Inevitably in some areas, particularly where the paint is thin or especially stubborn, the top coat can be lost through to the primer finish beneath. Here, a degree of compromise has to be reached, as it is all but

impossible not to rub through to the undercoat. This is further compounded by the fact that, during the aircraft's time in the Service and at Cranfield College, some areas of the original paint would have been worn, scratched or damaged as part of its routine existence. By observing, mapping, sketching or photographing individual areas the team was able to assess whether areas of missing paintwork dated from before 1963 or resulted from 'over-removal' on our part. This, in turn, allowed selected refinishing of our own over-removed areas, using specially matched paint applied very specifically, using a fine airbrush spray. Provided this was kept to an absolute minimum, it was considered acceptable to proceed in this way.

During the cleaning process, evidence of runs in the paint were also discovered. This immediately prompted suspicions that this under-layer of paintwork might not be factory original after all. Had the aircraft been more extensively resprayed than we had at first thought?

Very careful and light rubbing-down of these paint-run areas provided an answer to our question, and also allowed us to gain an understanding of how these components might have been handled during finishing at the factory. The runs were in the primer undercoat, not in the top coat. That

Engine installation on the Goodyear factory production line. Women undertook many engineering roles during the war years to ensure that aircraft production and quality stayed on target. Note that the aircraft in the background have engines fitted, whereas those in the foreground do not, suggesting that aircraft actually travelled backwards along the production line. (Goodyear Tire & Rubber)

The distinctive and immensely strong gull-wing centre section was the starting point for all Corsairs. This newly started British airframe is about to begin its swift backwards journey along the Goodyear production line, emerging as a flight-worthy aircraft in just a few weeks. *(Goodyear Tire & Rubber)*

would have proved little if it were not for the fact that the runs were at 90 degrees to the vertical; horizontal on the aircraft. If the cowling ring had never been removed and the paint runs were horizontal, the ring must have been sprayed with undercoat before it was fitted. The glossy blue finish bearing the factory stencil is also directly on top of this primer coat. It was also noteworthy that the runs flowed around the cowling in the direction from the greatest diameter towards the smallest diameter. Had the cowling been removed for respraying post-factory, it would have been very difficult and awkward to spray this rounded component resting in this orientation. The current theory is that, in the factory, they were possibly sprayed while suspended from their mounting brackets. This would have allowed relatively easy access to the whole shape and area for spraying, and any runs would have naturally formed in the direction of those on our cowling. Judging by the number of paint runs we were to discover, the spraying of primer coats seems to have been a haphazard treatment.

Immediately behind the forward cowling ring is the main set of four detachable engine access panels. These panels had already been removed to provide such access, as was their intended use. How often, though, are the engine covers or outer panels removed and ignored in the hurry to examine what is often considered to be 'the more interesting bit' underneath? What of the panels themselves? Should they not also be scrutinised for any interesting clues or references to the aircraft's history? Simply because many people might have touched, removed, altered or adjusted these panels, they may offer a better series of clues than the items concealed beneath.

The panels each cover approximately a quarter of the circumference of the engine and are marked 'top right', 'bottom right' and so on to allow for best fitting. These markings are handwritten in pencil on the inside faces, over the original primer (though on removal the panels were found to have been fitted to the aircraft in the incorrect sequence). Also, all of the panels are ink stamped with KD431, a manufacturer's part number and a recurring reference number, 2499, with a distinct style of ink printing block, strongly suggesting that the whole set was so marked during manufacture.

One exciting find on the inside of one panel was mathematical calculations and jottings, written in pencil. It is uncertain whether these relate to the aircraft build, later engine fitting/adjustments or something else, known only to whoever was responsible. I have often run the figures through my mind, intrigued as to their significance, but as yet can draw no conclusion.

During cleaning many details began to emerge that prompted much closer examination. *(FAAM)*

Inspection of the exterior of the outer panels showed that the same series of blue and blue/grey paint applications had been made as on the front cowling ring. Also evident under the blue/grey finish was a dirty, washed-out, grime-ingrained series of stripes. These handpainted marks, difficult to see on some areas of the panels, appeared to go in a variety of directions and made no sense at all until the panels were rearranged into their correct orientation and fitting sequence. Then, to our surprise and delight, the stripes formed themselves into the number sequence 431. The marking out of the numbering is very crude and roughly applied to both sides of the aircraft, giving every indication of being a temporary application. Furthermore, the numbers have been painted over in successive years with no obvious attempt to preserve their appearance. This number sequence had lain jumbled and hidden for years like an unsolved puzzle, waiting to be unravelled. What we were looking at was almost certainly the remains of the Goodyear factory identification numbering, and possibly the last original example of such left in existence.

Typically of American contract aircraft production of the time, the factory would have needed to distinguish easily between batch and contract numbers of aircraft rolling off the assembly line. Many factories, including Goodyear, adopted the practice of handpainting large, easily recognisable numbers on to the nose cowlings/panels for this purpose. For British contract aircraft it was normally the last three digits of the intended full serial number; in this case 431. This was invariably a

For many years the engine cowlings had been fitted out of sequence. Correct positioning allowed a riddle to be slowly solved, rather like an ancient puzzle. *(FAAM)*

temporary application, using paint that could easily be removed or painted over when the aircraft reached its intended unit.

The normal colour used for such identification on a dark-coloured aircraft was white (or a light colour). However, no traces of white paint could be found on the 431 marking. What appears to have happened is that the paint used for the marking has chemically reacted with, or in

This period picture of newly delivered Corsair KD300 clearly shows the ferry code '300' applied to the nose cowlings. These markings were for factory and delivery reference only, and were intended as temporary applications. *(FAAM)*

some way stained, the original blue paint finish on the panels. Although the white paint had degraded and disappeared over the years, it had left a very traceable outline on the panels, even leaving identifiable brush marks from the application process.

The next challenge was to clean the panels back to their original factory blue finish, leaving the very rare (possibly unique) 431 marking visible and

intact. For ease of working it was decided to refit the panels set into their correct positions on the aircraft. This would allow the best overall access to the working area, and also ensure that the whole outline of the 431 legend could be studied and accurately followed.

During cleaning, another series of markings or identifications was discovered. Each panel is held in place by a number of quick-release fasteners. One fastener on each of the panels (always in a corner position) was found to have a blue circle applied around it in paint (or ink). This, we eventually discovered, was common to all of the forward-position panels on the aircraft, but what was its purpose? There are two reasonable theories. It might have been some form of inspection process carried out in the factory, indicating that everything behind that particular panel had been inspected and approved. The weakness of this theory is that it could be seen as a fallible system, and does not explain why a corner fastener should always be chosen. Alternatively, the markings might refer to the recommended starting point to achieve best and most even fitting of the panel when affixing it to the aircraft. This theory is very logical, but as yet no factory evidence is available, nor have any aircraft fitters from the period provided any conclusive evidence.

Reference to photographs and written works on Corsairs, and communication with other museums and Corsair owners, again highlighted an important fact. Not only was this marking little understood, but it had almost certainly been removed from all other known Corsairs as a result of over-zealous refurbishment.

USING NUMBERS AS EVIDENCE

All aircraft carry certain identification numbers, build numbers, serial numbers etc. These can range in form from handpainted or stencilled numbers (like the '431' ferry code applied to the nose cowlings) to manufacturer's stamped metal plates. These are all dependent on the point of build or stage of fit the aircraft had reached when they were applied. Stencil-painted on to the inner face of the engine firewall (a standard position for such a marking) is the aircraft build or fabrication number, applied at the aircraft's initial build stage on the manufacturer's production line. In this case fabrication number 1871. This is individual to each aircraft, as is its Bureau number (the official US identification number), which for this aircraft is Bu No. 14862, and its British Service serial number, KD431. Unlike the squadron identification codes, these numbers remain unchanged throughout the aircraft's life.

The serial number, sometimes abbreviated to 431, appears hand-applied on many parts of the aircraft. However, the Bureau number has been deduced only by studying and calculating the recorded batches of Bureau numbers released from Goodyear factory records and the US Navy aircraft records list. This number should appear on the aircraft, usually stamped into a small aluminium plate riveted to the dashboard, but so far no physical evidence of the Bureau number has been found anywhere on the Corsair.

Ingrained with oil and dirt but still remaining after more than sixty years, this is the original hand-applied temporary aircraft ferry code, 431, from the factory production line. Its survival is remarkable. *(FAAM)*

The devil is in the detail. Although reference sources give white as the normal colour for the cowling-fastener reference circles, on KD431 they are unusual in being blue. These highlighters appear throughout the aircraft, one fastener on every removable panel being marked this way, even when a panel has only two fasteners. *(FAAM)*

Fabrication number 1871 stencilled (upside-down) on the engine-compartment firewall of KD431. This factory build fabrication number tallies with the aircraft's serial number, but other numbers on the aircraft do not. *(FAAM)*

Many mysteries and riddles have been solved concerning the aircraft's history, but KD431 has not given up all her secrets – yet. *(FAAM)*

One other number that remains constant for all aircraft of any given batch is the government contract number. This is the overall code number given to the factory by the government under which the aircraft contract is listed. For all Goodyear-built Corsairs the government contract number was 1871.

One coincidence that caused confusion for many weeks while the numbering, dating and exact mark and type of our aircraft was being researched was the fact that, of all the Corsairs built, only one had build number 1871, the same as the overall government contract number, and it was our aircraft. This is a small and insignificant fact, but it is amusing that, of nearly 12,000 Corsair number sequences, the only matching one should be that of our survivor.

If that were not coincidence enough, the discovery of a mathematical calculation pencilled on the inside face of a cowling panel added more intrigue and mystery. The calculation reads: 1871 – [minus] 1440 = 431. On the face of it there is nothing very unusual about that basic arithmetical subtraction, but analyse the numbers more closely and the intrigue develops. Knowing that 1871 is the build/fabrication number of our aircraft, the number 1440 must surely relate to the earlier aircraft that was given that fabrication number. Checking this against the Goodyear fabrication log revealed a bizarre coincidence indeed. Fabrication number 1440 relates to a US Navy FG-1A Corsair in an earlier delivery batch of Goodyear Corsairs and tallying with Bu No. (equivalent US serial number) 14431. Our aircraft, serial number 431, is 431 spaces behind US Bureau number Corsair Bu No. 14431.

Whoever used the fabrication numbers 1871 and 1440 to do the sum must surely have been analysing this strange coincidence; but to what end or significance? And why scribble it on the inner face of a cowling? Why would they be comparing the fabrication numbers (and hence respective serial/Bureau numbers) of a British and US aircraft that in theory at least should have left the factory more than a month apart? What made that person notice or recognise this numerical coincidence?

The fabrication log lists batches of numbers, so a quick glance will not readily reveal this number alignment. A subtraction exercise is required to spot it. Also, unless your mental arithmetic is very sharp, you have to count back in the fabrication number column and then transfer to the Bureau number column to continue the check. Having noticed it is one thing, but why perform the calculation on our aircraft? The mystery deepens.

The handwritten pencil calculation on the inside of the upper engine cowling. This basic arithmetic subtraction appears to link the FAAM Corsair, serial number KD431, with US Navy Corsair Bureau number (equivalent to serial number) 14431, 431 units away on the production line. *(FAAM)*

WHAT MARK OF CORSAIR WAS KD431?

There now seemed to be a contradiction, depending upon which source document we were using. Corsair KD431 appeared in the Goodyear Aircraft Company log of aircraft fabrication numbers in the build number batch 1705–2000, clearly making it a significantly rarer FG-1A, and not an FG-1D as we had long believed. Possibly only one other FG-1A still existed as a whole aircraft, in the US Marine Corps Museum at Quantico, Virginia, in the USA, and this was believed to have lost much of its originality owing to recent refinishing for display purposes. However, the US Navy Bureau numbers log lists our aircraft as an FG-1D. Corsair KD431 was becoming more interesting by the minute, both as a study subject and, more significantly, as an historic object.

Handpainted on the supercharger intake ducts within the engine bay is the number 1883, indicating that parts from the Corsair of that build number had at some stage been fitted to our aircraft. It would be easy (and wrong) to assume that this substitution of parts occurred during service. Certainly part swapping in the field happened when a justifiable need arose, particularly in an emergency or in time of war. However, this was an unusual component to need to change, unless more damage had been caused in the immediate area. Moreover, all of the fasteners holding the ducts in place showed no sign of disturbance, or of scratching of the factory applied primer coat that would have been unavoidable during such an operation. Build number 1883 would have been twelve places behind our aircraft on the Goodyear production line, theoretically making its service serial KD444. A check of Service records showed that KD444 was attached to 1850 Sqn and was not operated in close association with 1835 or 768 Sqns. All of the evidence pointed to these components having been fitted to our aircraft on the manufacturer's production line, with no attempt to cancel the numbering from the associated donor aircraft.

The reason for this substitution can only be guessed. Why were the parts taken from an aircraft twelve spaces behind in the line, and what happened to 1871's respective components? What this does demonstrate, however, is that on wartime production lines components were drawn from a variety of sources to ensure that the lines kept flowing.

More importantly for us, fabrication number 1883 (KD444) appeared to be for an FG-1A. Confirmation of this detail would be of great importance to us in helping to prove the exact mark of our aircraft.

The supercharger intake duct is hand-marked 1883 RH (right hand), clear evidence that components were swapped and changed with those of other aircraft on the production line. *(FAAM)*

STOP AND THINK

Once this task was completed it was time to stop and evaluate all that we had uncovered to date. Stop-and-think time, as already mentioned, is of the utmost importance during all stages of work. It was also essential to gather the team, examine evidence, and exercise a whole series of thought processes and theories based on what we could see and what we were finding. Golden rule number one was that no person's theories were ridiculed or laughed at. Even the most absurd theories could spark a new thought process or point in the direction of something that had been missed. Inviting interested people into the hangar who have previously not been connected with the aircraft or the project can also prove very useful. It has the benefit of providing a viewpoint from someone with no preconceived ideas of the aircraft itself or the work being undertaken, and sometimes results in a new thought process being generated. In addition, watching (and comparing) how people move around the aircraft can prompt new thoughts. Where they naturally put a hand or reach for; where they stand, step to or lean; what might have caused a dent or a series of marks or scratches? The whole project was a constant evaluation exercise that sometimes seemed nearer to detective work or forensic science, which is what I believe good restoration technique should include. Recording information is equally important. Photographing each stage of the work, making notes and sketches, jotting down ideas or theories and noting any verbal recollections from people previously associated with the aircraft. All of this information steadily builds into a vital database that would be impossible to remember accurately but can be laid out, re-arranged and studied in a variety of useful ways.

Thorough and accurate research is also of paramount importance, and one quite simply cannot do enough.

So what had we got so far, and what was our understanding of it? The forward portion of the aircraft had now been thoroughly cleaned and examined, and all of the details and witness marks recorded:

1. The propeller, apparently in its original paint finish and bearing damage that might date from 1945.
   An accident record card that might well prove this beyond doubt.
2. The engine, looking remarkably original, complete and undisturbed, with the delicate paper ticket still affixed to the mounting frame recess.
3. The front cowling ring with original factory stencilling and horizontal paint runs.
4. The set of four engine panels still bearing the remains of what appeared to be the Goodyear factory recognition code 431.
5. The ink stamps on all internal panel faces that match in both style and numbering.
6. The blue identification circles applied around the panel fasteners.

49

A view showing the ferry code on the port side of the engine cowlings. At this stage the whole nose section of the aircraft was beginning to give every indication of being completely factory original from 1944, right down to the paintwork and markings. *(FAAM)*

Finding any one of these details still remaining on the aircraft would have been interesting in its own right. Finding them all on the same aircraft, so closely linked and related, and appearing within the first 6ft of fuselage to be examined, was very special. The fact that such a mass of apparently original features still existed was beginning to take the aircraft beyond being very interesting, and making it historically significant and important.

The area connected with and around the engine of an aircraft often attracts the greatest amount of work during its Service life. Wings are not normally changed, tails are often fixtures, and cockpit modifications are usually minor. The engine region is very different. Servicing schedules for the engine dictate the regular removal of inspection panels. Likewise, related components will be adjusted, modified or replaced as necessary. This can in turn lead to many variations from the factory original, even panels from a different aircraft sometimes being fitted.

The fact that KD431 appeared to have so many original features (even paintwork details) on what is normally regarded as the area of greatest servicing activity (and likelihood of change) suggested that the rest of the aircraft was equally original. If this was so, it might well prove to be the most complete and original surviving example of a Corsair. Indeed, it could be one of the most original Second World War aircraft still in close to factory condition. There was every reason to proceed with the project using the same system and method, but now we would be examining any given working area even more closely.

Considering our increasing excitement, it would be all too easy to rush headlong into the task, risking irreversible damage. Very often, with any given task, it is quite normal to feel (or measure) the pace quickening with the natural excitement and momentum of the job. This had to be kept under tight control, and it sometimes seemed that the project was slowing down. The team had to stay focused, keen, observant and accurate, but not become demoralised by the apparent lack of progress. Techniques were constantly being modified to suit a particular area or need, and many weeks would often pass without any obvious change. This very difficult balancing act was made immeasurably easier by the support and far-sighted view of the upper management level at the museum, and by the ability of the small and dedicated team who appreciated what the end result would mean.

FUSELAGE PANELS FORWARD OF THE COCKPIT

Arranged around the periphery of the fuselage, ahead of the accessory drive access panels, is a set of cooling gills. These small flaps are linked by an operating cable that in turn connects with a control linkage to the cockpit. This enables the pilot to regulate the airflow through the engine bay by opening or closing the gills as necessary. Thorough cleaning and examination of the gills showed that they comprised a complete set, correctly fitted into position and attached to the operating linkage. On the inside of each gill panel was ink-stamped the factory reference KD431. There were no missing or differently stamped gill panels, and all of the ink stamping matched that of the forward engine panels. It appeared that this complete set was still in position as per original factory fit.

Most of the fuselage panels and cowlings on this portion of the aircraft appear to be original and correctly fitted, some having the now familiar KD431 reference, ink-block marked in the same way as the forward engine panels. However, the original left-hand-side (port) accessory drive access panel was missing, having been replaced by a poor-quality sheet-metal panel. The replacement had no frame or ribs, and was poorly fashioned to cover the hole left by the original panel. It is very doubtful that this cover dates from the aircraft's time in service. Hasty repairs and modifications under wartime conditions are not unknown, but this panel was not of the quality and suitability required for an airworthy airframe.

Photographs depicting the aircraft during its time at Cranfield College show what appears to be some form of hydraulic rig (manufactured

Corsair KD431 on display at a Cranfield College open day in 1954. The remote hydraulic rig has been fitted to the port side of the aircraft to enable the wing-folding mechanism to be operated. *(J. Halley, MBE)*

locally?) fitted to this side of the aircraft. This adaptation evidently resulted in the removal of the accessory drive access panel. Other photographs show the aircraft parked outside the college about 1963, with the panel still missing, apparently awaiting collection by the Royal Navy for transportation to its new home at Yeovilton. Judging from the state of neglect of the aircraft in photographs, there is reason to believe that the original panel was removed at Cranfield and possibly lost, modified or scrapped during the seventeen years it spent there. It is possible that the replacement panel was quickly fabricated at Cranfield to replace the missing item, but the author believes that it is more likely to have been made shortly after the aircraft's arrival at Yeovilton.

The right-hand-side (starboard) accessory panel is an original panel (factory stamped KD431), and is fixed into position with the correct type of fasteners. This panel also houses the aperture for accessing the stowage box for the explosive cartridges used for starting the engine when a Coffman-type starter unit is fitted. Of immediate interest was the discovery that the access door had been riveted permanently closed, though the cartridge stowage box was still fitted.

Removal of the whole panel resulted in several other very interesting finds. The aircraft had originally been designed to be equipped for cartridge starting of the engine. (An explosive round, rather like a large shotgun cartridge, was discharged into a specially designed starter unit. This caused the starter to engage the engine with sufficient power to turn it over and effect a start.) However, this particular Corsair had been fitted with an updated electrical starting unit that dispensed with the need for the cartridge starter. It is not clear when this modification was carried out. However, unlike other small factory additions or modifications on the aircraft, the rivets used to secure the panel had not been finished with either a primer coat or top coat of paint. There is evidence of yellow painted dots, hand-applied to the blue paintwork immediately beneath these rivet heads, suggesting that the positioning of these rivets was a roughly gauged in-service modification. Also, the slots in the heads of the two quick-release fasteners on this panel showed signs of having been used, and the paintwork on the edge of this access panel showed signs of wear. It is reasonable to suspect, therefore, that this panel was regularly opened and used for at least part of the aircraft's Service life, to access the spare-cartridge stowage. Accurate factory records detailing when such changes or modifications were introduced might confirm whether the aircraft left the factory with a cartridge or electric starting device fitted. However, the evidence and witness marks point strongly towards this being an in-service modification.

The external face of the panel above this access panel bears the remains of some stencilled lettering originally applied in white. The lettering is not clear enough to be read in full, but its proximity to the access panel indicates that it may be a form of instruction or procedure for operating the starter unit. What is left of the instruction reads:

.... **ON** ....
INSERT ....
.... **OFF** ....

Remains of the factory-applied instruction relating to use of the oil tank heater. Certain words have been highlighted, probably by Royal Navy air fitters on 1835 or 768 Sqn. *(FAAM)*

The lettering is in a similar size and font to that of equivalent markings on other panels, which suggests that it was a factory application. However, the words 'ON' and 'OFF' have clearly been handpainted over in red paint to highlight and emphasise this part of the instruction. This freehand addition gives the impression of being a later, in-service alteration.

Close inspection of the oil tank (housed beneath this main accessory drive panel, and only visible after the panel was removed) revealed a paper ticket, varnished to the oil tank, immediately below the filler point. The writing on this now very fragile ticket was barely legible, but careful study revealed the instruction:

**SWITCH SOCKET MUST NOT BE TO ON
UNTIL HEATER HAS BEEN INSERTED INTO
TANK & MUST BE SWITCHED OFF BEFORE
HEATER IS REMOVED FROM TANK**

Only just legible, this handwritten paper ticket, varnished to the aircraft's oil tank, is the origin of the instruction relating to the oil tank heater. *(FAAM)*

Many aircraft are fitted with a system that allows a remote heater element to be safely inserted into the oil tank on cold days. The purpose of this is to prevent the oil becoming too viscous, therefore risking damage to a cold engine on start-up.

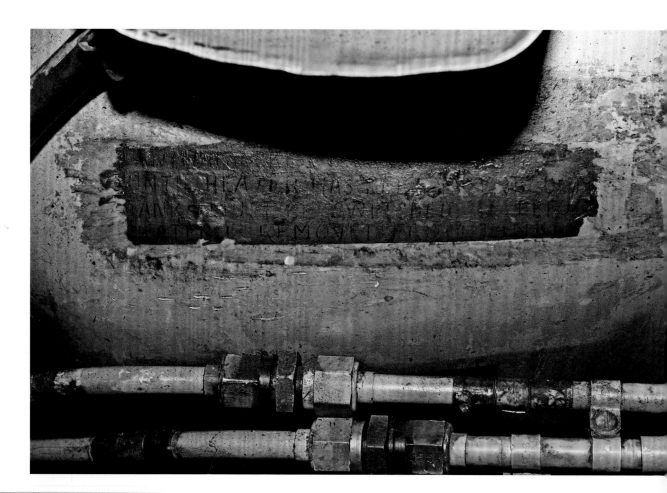

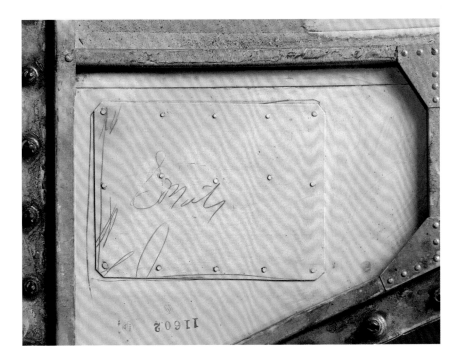

The word 'OFF' in this instruction is also highlighted in red, and the author is sure that the painted instruction on the exterior of the main panel refers to this fuller version on the oil tank. While it was important and interesting to discover the paper ticket, and to be able to decipher it and make this link, it also clearly demonstrated how easily one could be fooled by assuming the meaning of a piece of evidence purely because of its positioning; in this case the incorrect association of the painted instruction with the starter unit.

Of great interest, on the inside of the main accessory drive access panel, is an aluminium plate approximately 8in × 6in × ⅛in thick, riveted to the skin of the main panel. This plate, and its positioning, purpose and significance, are to date a complete mystery. The plate is affixed to the lower rear corner of the panel, on the inside face, by fifteen rivets. These rivets have been poorly aligned and spaced, giving the impression that the layout was gauged by eye rather than accurately measured. The position of this plate has been sketched freehand in pencil on top of the main panel's primer finish. Moreover, the plate itself has been very crudely cut from a larger piece of aluminium sheet that was apparently already primer-coated, as the pencil marks are on top of this finish. There is little or no accuracy about the whole job, neither the marking-out or cutting lines having been adhered to. The rivets and type of rivet forming used appear to match the surrounding factory riveting on other panels in size, type and form, and the plate is also spray-finished in a primer coat exactly matching the surrounding factory finishes.

To add to the intrigue and mystery, the plate bears what appears to be a fairly large, stylised handwritten signature (also in pencil). It is difficult to be sure, but the signature could be 'Smith' or 'Smity'.

This signature is on top of the primer coat, and the primer coat covers the cut edges of the plate in some places, suggesting that some attempt has been made to prime this area after the cutting of the plate). One of the fifteen rivet holes pierces exactly a part of the signature, strongly indicating that the signature was applied to the plate before it was riveted to the main panel. The remains of what appear to be other writing and rough marking-out lines can be seen along two edges of the plate. This suggests that these markings were made on the larger sheet before the smaller plate was cut out; hence the cut lines slice through these markings. It seems reasonable to suggest that the signature was applied to the plate before the riveting process, because the rivet hole pierces the pencil stroke of the signature. Whether the signature existed on the original sheet before the plate was cut out, or was applied later by the person responsible for the job, is unknown. There is no evidence of the outer panel having been punctured or damaged, and no obvious reason for an extra plate in this position. The corner positioning does not tally with the need for extra strength in what is already the strongest area of the panel, which again needed no obvious repair. The crudeness is completely contrary to all normally accepted aircraft fitting practices. The primer finish (including the primer finish on the rivet heads beneath the factory blue top finish) and riveting itself suggest a factory fitting, but by whom, what for, and why, are still mysteries. It is hard to imagine why someone would wish to sign

The position of the aluminium patch, looking from the outside of the panel (the heads of the fifteen poorly spaced rivets are just visible). With no obvious damage or hole to repair, the purpose of this patch remains a mystery. *(FAAM)*

such a poorly performed piece of sheet-metalwork, or why they would not be satisfied with just signing on the inside face of the panel, if it were their intention to mark this aircraft in such a way. An 8in × 6in plate, held on by fifteen rivets, seems excessive as a way of personalising an aircraft, and it is hard to imagine such an operation being approved by an aircraft inspector, either in the factory or in service. Its function remains unknown, but the following possible explanations are being considered:

1. A repair patch; but there is no obvious damage or crack to the panel skin.
2. A strengthening patch; but this corner of the panel is already well braced and framed. Moreover, the panel is not a stressed skin, and therefore does not need to be self-supporting.
3. A personalised nameplate; unlikely, based on the size of the plate, the number of fixing rivets, and the position of rivets and signature.
4. An anti-rub/chafing panel; unlikely, as there is nothing immediately behind the panel to suggest the need for protection. Preventing the likelihood of chafing in the first place would be normal aircraft practice. Also, the tails of the rivets on the inside face now present a chafing hazard themselves.
5. A practice repair exercise by a trainee; most unlikely. Why would such a practice be necessary or allowed on a new undamaged aircraft?
6. A weakness in this area of the panel that required a modification; this cannot be compared with the left-hand (port) panel, as it is missing. However, comparing notes with other Corsair owners has yet to identify any similar practice. It is also difficult to imagine why such crude/poor practice was allowed or approved, as such poor rivet alignment and crudeness of fit could in some ways be seen as detrimental to the strength of the panel.

OIL FILLER ACCESS

Another small door allowing entry to the engine oil filler point is also housed within the main accessory drive access panel. Careful cleaning revealed that several attempts had been made to apply and modify markings to this door, both in factory stencilling and free-hand painting. The original factory markings take the form of white ink/paint letters similar to those found on other areas of the aircraft. The door is identified as the oil filler access by the words 'OIL FILLER'. This lettering has firstly been applied, part-way down the door, to one side and off-level, using the now familiar factory stencil or block-stamp marking method. Interestingly it has been reapplied at the top of the door in a much neater fashion, but still in the factory-type print block/stencilling. This pattern of finding

poorly applied then reapplied, better factory markings was to become familiar on much of the aircraft. Re-marking or updating of information panels during service is quite common, but this quite obvious (and repeated) practice of reapplying an instruction in a neater fashion over the top of an earlier, badly applied instruction seems poor practice during the manufacturing process.

The capacity of the oil tank is marked as '21.5 IMP. GALLS' (Imperial gallons), again in the factory-type lettering. However, the words 'IMP. GALLS' have also been applied twice, first off-line and crooked and then better positioned and straight. In addition to the factory stencilling, a crudely handpainted 'T/XX' has been applied across the centre of the door and covering a portion of the original factory lettering. This marking has been applied first in black paint and then reapplied (carefully mapping the first application) in white paint. This appears to have been a later in-service modification to the door markings, and presumably refers to the type or grade of oil that is to be used for replenishing the system (as yet it is unknown if the grade reference is T/XX or T/20).

It is worth noting that the capacity indicated on the door (21.5 IMP.GALLS) does not tally with the manufacturer's transfer applied to the oil filler cap itself, which reads '24½ GALS'. For a tank of such volume, 2¾ gallons represents a considerable difference in capacity and, even considering that a US gallon is only four-fifths of an Imperial gallon, the sums do not add up. It is unclear, therefore, why these two factory-applied references do not agree.

On the top of the oil tank has been written '125 # torque', hand-applied in pencil. Torque references and measurements refer to the tightness applied to nuts, bolts and screw-threaded components during assembly. The most likely Imperial measurements would be 125lb.ft or lb.in, but either would appear to be too high for safe use on any of the thread sizes visible in this immediate area. A torque loading of 12.5 lb.ft or lb.in would be more in keeping with the thread sizes associated with the tank fittings, but no decimal point is visible. Another possibility is that the 125 relates to a numerical system used by and known only to American manufacturers. The location of the writing suggests that it was applied before the tank was fully connected and plumbed in, because it is directly beneath a main oil delivery pipe and not easily accessible.

As with many of these details, it is not always what is written that is of interest. Where or why it was written (or allowed to be written or marked) can often be a far more fascinating subject. All of this information, often insignificant on its own, contributes to the whole story surrounding the object, and how the people working on it thought, acted and made notes, adjustments, modifications or even mistakes. This type of close detail-by-detail study also sets a benchmark for similar objects, studies and comparisons. The individual details may apply only to this aircraft, but the overall result of such a study provides a known, and in many areas proven, start point for the study of other American-built aircraft of the same era. This in turn provides a database of information from which accurate and meaningful studies and comparisons can be made with any other aircraft of the period.

This instruction placard was repositioned by a fraction of an inch, masked over and then sprayed during factory assembly. However, the masking tape was not removed after the process, leaving the instruction obscured. *(FAAM)*

The door is held closed by two quick-release fasteners on its lower edge, the forward of the two bearing a blue circle like those on the main cowling fasteners. Opening the door revealed further examples of reapplication and fits concerning this component, with no immediate explanations. On the inside face an instruction plate approximately 5in × 2in is affixed inverted by four small screws, so that when the door is opened upwards it reads correctly. This plate, black with white lettering, refers to the extent to which the oil tank should be filled in relation to the amount of gasoline in the aircraft's fuel tanks. This, presumably, is linked to the fact that the aircraft has an oil-dilution system, allowing a small amount of fuel to be mixed with the engine oil, under the pilot's control, just before the aircraft's engine is stopped, thus enabling a slightly diluted oil mix to be fed to the engine on re-start. This system was particularly useful in extremely cold conditions, or when used in conjunction with the oil heater system. However, levels of fuel and oil within the system had to be monitored to prevent over-filling, back-filling or vapour build-up in certain parts of the system.

The plate had been masked over with brown adhesive masking paper and the inside face of the door resprayed in factory-finish primer. Careful removal of the plate revealed that the door had already been spray-primed before the plate was affixed, and that the finish was in good sound condition. In addition to this seemingly unnecessary treatment, an extra set of screw holes for affixing the plate had been drilled. This unused set of holes matched, in perfect alignment, the holes on the plate, but it is a mystery why they were not used and the plate was repositioned a fraction of an inch higher. In addition, the masking paper, still coated in factory primer overspray, had never been fully removed, so the instruction, and its important message, remained largely covered and unreadable. All of this appeared to be factory-performed work.

HYDRAULIC FLUID – FILLER ACCESS AND TANK

Situated at the uppermost point of the fuselage, forward of the cockpit windscreen, is a small access door allowing entry to the hydraulic-fluid reservoir. This door is held closed by two quick-release fasteners, positioned along its forward edge. One of these fasteners has been marked with a blue ink/paint circle like the aircraft's other cowlings and access panels. Applied to the door in white paint/ink stencilling is information regarding the capacity of the reservoir and the fluid recommended for use. Again, this stamped or stencilled placard has initially been applied in poor alignment with the door outline, and then reapplied more neatly and centrally.

Removal of the entire panel housing this access door exposes the hydraulic reservoir itself. This tank is fixed into position on a mounting frame and appears to be as fitted in the factory. Situated next to the hydraulic reservoir is the bracket and framework to support the hydraulic

Whether '1st coat' refers to the primer coat on the hydraulic tank or to the whole aircraft is unknown. The component, and the surrounding inner-fuselage area, has only one coat of primer, and a second coat would have covered this instruction. Moreover, no other areas of the aircraft have been marked similarly or with successive second- or third-coat markings. (FAAM)

pump or accumulator, though this component is missing. It seems likely that the removal of this component dates from the aircraft's time at Cranfield, where a temporary hydraulic rig was attached to the aircraft for ground operation of some of the systems.

One point is worthy of note. On the rear of the tank, printed on top of its primer coat in purple ink, is the reference '1st coat'. This marking has not been found anywhere else on the aircraft, but appears to relate to the primer finish. Whether this refers to the entire aircraft's primer finish, or only to that of the tank, is unknown. The primer, however, is the only coat of paint applied to this particular item.

WATER HEADER TANK

Positioned immediately in front of the hydraulic reservoir is a water reservoir. This tank contained a small amount of water that was deliberately injected into the engine as part of the fuel mixing and combustion process. Adding atomised water into the combustion mixture at high engine revolutions and maximum power increased the volume and effectiveness of the combustion, especially at high altitude, and also provided a degree of cooling within the combustion chamber under these extreme conditions.

The tank was manufactured by the Lennox Furnace Company of Columbus, Ohio, USA, and still has its manufacturer's original (now very fragile) transfer applied to the rear face. Among the details given on the transfer is the tank's specified capacity of 4.9 US gallons. In addition to this, positioned immediately above the transfer and on the paintwork of the tank is an ink-stamped specification reading '4.1 IMP Galls'. This refers to the British equivalent tank capacity. However, it is not known

whether this additional information was applied in the factory to aircraft destined for British use, at the British aircraft pre-delivery centre (Roosevelt Field, New York), or at unit level after delivery. The fact that the information was applied using a purpose-made ink block or stencil implies a factory application, and suggests that Goodyear was prepared to manufacture blocks/stencils and reapply information, rather than require companies such as Lennox to manufacture alternative transfers.

The filler cap had been handpainted red, with the screw-tightening slot highlighted in white. This poorly-applied highlight appears to be more in keeping with an in-service modification.

FUEL TANK COVER PANELS

Immediately in front of the cockpit windscreen is a large panel that forms the top curve of the fuselage. Beneath it is housed the aircraft's main fuel tank, situated behind the engine and directly in front of the pilot. Its capacity is 197 Imperial gallons.

Large, heavy items such as engines, fuel tanks and armament need to be kept close to the aircraft's c.g. (usually within the wing chord) to ensure good flying characteristics. Everything cannot fit into this one space, so lighter objects, such as the pilot, may have to be moved. The Corsair is one of the best examples of engine and fuel tank sizes forcing the pilot's position rearward, to such an extent that the resulting limited forward view made flying the aircraft from a ship's deck a daunting task. The nose length, from the tip of the propeller hub to the centre of the pilot's seat, is 16ft 3in. This was 3ft longer than the similar distance on the British-manufactured Supermarine Seafire, the nose length of which was already considered too long by some pilots.

Aircraft panels and cowlings immediately in front of the cockpit, and in the pilot's direct line of vision, are very often painted with matt-finish paint, or even matt black, to eliminate sunlight glare from this surface, which would otherwise cause a serious distraction to the pilot. This was not so in the case of KD431. Careful removal of the more recent coat of paint revealed that the panels in this area were painted in glossy sea blue, like all of the cowlings and panels uncovered thus far. Any suspicion that the panel might have had a more thorough repaint on its arrival at Yeovilton foundered on the discovery of more ink-block-applied factory stencils in this area, on top of the gloss sea blue paint.

The main fuel tank filler point is positioned centrally at the top of this panel. In front of the filler cap, white ink-block-applied lettering in the now-familiar factory style reads:

SERVICE AIRPLANE WITH 100–130 FUEL

This refers to the octane rating of the fuel to be used in the aircraft. However, beneath the letters SE of the word SERVICE are traces of a word or the letters 'I T' applied to the panel, also in the ink-block style. Unfortunately the wording has worn away too much in this area to enable its meaning to be determined.

Immediately below this factory-applied wording is the repeated instruction:

100 OCT ONLY

Locally applied squadron alterations to markings jockey for position with original markings. This area around the main fuel tank filler is a superb example of how factory-applied markings were often altered and highlighted for daily squadron use. *(FAAM)*

This has been crudely applied by brush, in red paint and in larger freehand letters than the neat white factory stencilling immediately above. This was almost certainly an in-service addition, but whether the intention was to replace eroding factory lettering or emphasise the specific octane rating is unknown. One theory is that only 100-octane fuel might have been readily available in wartime Britain, and that this instruction could have been applied to avoid confusion.

The main fuel tank filler cap had itself been spray-finished in red paint, and a red ring (4in in diameter and ½in thick) had been spray-applied to the panel around the outside of the filler cap to highlight its location.

Below the filler cap is more factory-applied lettering, in the form of a stencil or ink-block marking. This is also red, and is intended as a cautionary notice. Unfortunately the lettering has worn away to such a degree that the whole instruction cannot now be read. Again, this printed instruction has the appearance of a factory-applied item, and from its positioning seems to refer to the fuel filling procedure. However, without confirmation from a technical manual this cannot be ascertained. Remember the error of assumption on the previous panel! What is left of the instruction reads:

.... AN ON FILLING ....
.... TO FILLER NECK SEALING ....

Between this instruction and immediately in front of the aircraft's windscreen there is an earthing point. This externally mounted plug socket was used to attach an earthing (or ground) lead from the aircraft to a safe remote earthing point during refuelling procedures, or while carrying out electrical maintenance on the aircraft. This plug socket is identified by white lettering (reading 'GROUND HERE' and an arrow symbol) like the other markings, and has again been applied twice. The restamp appears to use exactly the same stamp as the first, and is only a fraction of an inch different in positioning. This reapplication (as with all of the other block stamps found thus far) actually makes the instructions less legible and presents, in some cases, the potential for misunderstanding and, hence, mishandling or damaging the aircraft. The lower right-hand side of this panel also houses a handhold slot to aid access to the starboard side of the aircraft, and the identification for this has also been applied twice, apparently with the same block or stamp. Although the first application might not have been central or level on any particular panel, it does not appear to be so badly misplaced as to warrant a reapplication. Indeed, the reapplication only serves to confuse the instruction, and would presumably have taken longer to apply. Whether these reapplications were an attempt by an individual to improve a situation or an instruction from some level of quality assurance is unknown. One often hears the emphatic advice from some sources that 'an aircraft would never leave the factory looking like that', or that 'they would never have done that'. Well, here is the evidence and proof that they sometimes must have done. For whatever reason, the whole of the front of the aircraft has been double-stamped with the white ink-block instructions.

An electrical earth-bonding point and a hand-hold access flap provide further curious examples of factory stencilling that has been applied twice. This seems to have been done everywhere on the aircraft. *(FAAM)*

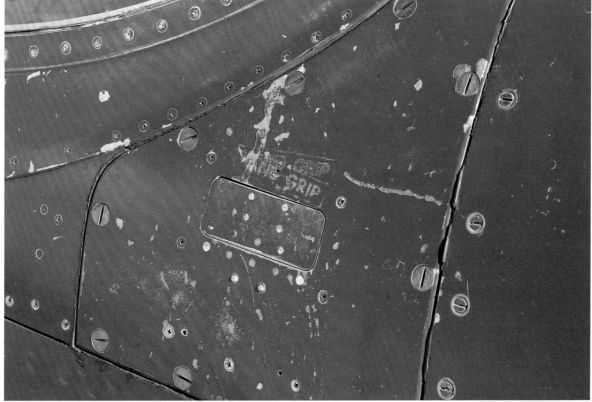

STOP AND THINK AGAIN

The whole forward section of fuselage, from the propeller back as far as the cockpit, had now been returned to its original 1944 paint finish. What was all of this telling and showing us, and of what importance was it? It was time to stop, think and re-evaluate all that we had so far uncovered. What had we achieved? Was it worth continuing using the same methods? Was it worth continuing at all?

The aircraft could quite easily have had extensive areas of paint re-moved, either by abrasive or wet chemical stripping, in 1963 when the superficial tidy-up finish was applied. This, however, was proving to be very much not the case. Furthermore, we had been able to uncover and

preserve not only the original paint finish, but also factory-applied transfers, stencilled instructions and witness marks relating to factory production techniques. In addition, the in-service witness marks were revealing their own story. The result was proving to be far more interesting than we had hoped, and even at this early stage there was a growing sense of excitement regarding what we might ultimately reveal; a time capsule.

By this stage the whole team was becoming proficient at removing dark blue/grey paint from on top of dark blue paint. The techniques were broadly the same on most areas of the panel work, but fine adjustments to rubbing-compound mix or the pressure used during removal were constantly being made. Paint thickness varied enormously, both on the original factory finish and the 1963 finish. This, along with panel shape or curvature, presented constantly changing terrain that at times seemed to present itself as one long experiment. However, we had now returned a sizeable area of the aircraft to its original state, and felt confident that the same could be done with the remainder.

A few small test areas on the wings, tail and rear fuselage were also exposing what we now recognised as the original factory finish. This seemed to exist on all the remaining areas of the aircraft, concealed beneath a non-original coat of paint. Studying technical manuals and photographs to locate stencilled instructions or transfers yielded little accurate information. Our own scrupulous observation, careful work and constantly improving technique was all that could be relied upon. Indeed, at this point we began to realise just how important the work would be if we could complete it fully and successfully. The lack of detailed information in the technical manuals and photographs (to the level that we needed and were uncovering) was making us realise that we were compiling a document that did not exist; a record of the complete disposition, over the entire aircraft, of all the markings applied by the manufacturer and modified by the first squadrons to take charge of the aeroplane. This should not have been such an unusual revelation, but research was showing us that virtually no other Second World War aircraft remained in such total and completely original condition. It most certainly was worth continuing the work.

At this point another decision had to be made. In which direction should we go next? Should we continue along the fuselage's length as a team, or divide and work on several different areas? Working on

Evidence of wear and tear. Countless air fitters and service crews have left their marks while clambering on to the wings, opening panels and rubbing against paintwork. (FAAM)

the same area of fuselage was becoming crowded and awkward at times, but would splitting the workforce (and focus) be detrimental to identifying and understanding the vital details that we were uncovering? As a team we decided that tackling separate areas was preferable. We agreed that all areas were to be treated with equal importance, that work rate was dictated only by technique and quality of result, and that maximum preserved original detail was the goal. This was not a race to see who could uncover the greatest area in the shortest time.

The only problem with this approach was recording the large number of details that were now emerging from several areas at once. Consequently, much of my time became occupied with recording this information, and less with hands-on work on the aircraft. Some might say this was very lucky (or convenient), but despite all of the interest in the recording, checking and research, I did miss the thrill of being the one to uncover some rare or unique details, believed to have been extinct for the last sixty years or so. The move to work on separate areas also seemed to produce a tighter, more focused and enquiring team. Stop-and-think time was now turning into constant open questions, comparisons and evaluations between each area of work in progress. The team was beginning to look at the aircraft as a whole and examine how their detail related to that being uncovered in another area, what they understood from it, and how it affected what they did next.

WINGS

Blending into the fuselage at the mid-point is the aircraft's wing, which differs from those of many aircraft in its gull-wing configuration. This arrangement was essential to raise the fuselage (and hence the engine and propeller) sufficiently clear of the ground while retaining a short, strong undercarriage leg.

The wings were manufactured by Briggs Industries of Detroit, USA; another example of wartime mass production being spread among a number of large factories to produce components and subassemblies for one main aircraft production line.

Briggs Industries grew out of a series of amalgamations and changes. In 1907 Walter O. Briggs was manager of the Everitt Carriage Trimming Company, which belonged to Mr Byron Everitt. That year Everitt sold his company to Briggs, and this marked the start of the Briggs Manufacturing Company at 1551 Harper, Detroit, USA. The factory, scene of the worst fire in Detroit's history in 1927, claiming twenty-seven lives, produced and painted automobile bodies and parts for companies such as the Packard, Chrysler, Dodge and Paige-Detroit motor car companies. By the 1940s the company had its own aero-engineering division, producing components and subassemblies to government contract specification, including Corsair outer wings.

The wings of KD431 carry original Briggs Manufacturing Company plates, stamped as follows with three references, indicating their suitability

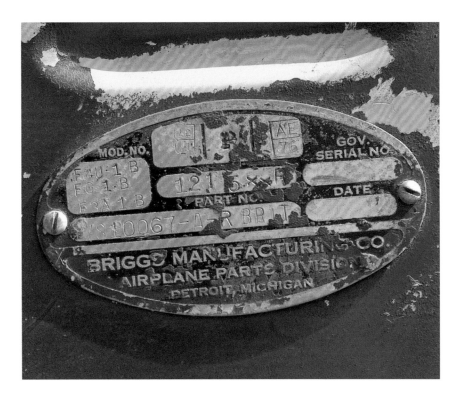

for fitting to British-contract Corsairs from any one of the three manufacturing companies concerned:

Model   F4U-1-BRIT (Vought-manufactured models)
             F3A-1-BRIT (Brewster-manufactured models)
             FG-1-BRIT (Goodyear-manufactured models).

The wings of British-contract Corsairs differed from those of the US-contract aircraft, and needed to be clearly distinguished. A shortened wingtip (referred to later) was the most obvious of the differences.

Clearly Briggs was involved at a stage in manufacture when the Vought, Brewster and Goodyear companies were still engaged in Corsair production, and were being supplied with British specification wings for the relevant contract batches. It is not known whether Briggs continued to stamp wings with the Brewster F3A-1 reference after the Brewster company ceased to function, for continued retro-replacement on in-service Brewster-built aircraft.

The wings are handed and marked as such, each respective wing part number being prefixed with an 'L' or 'R' to indicate left or right. The numbers are hand-stamped into the web spanning the root end of the main spar, but here again inconsistencies in detail and numbering were found. The port wing carries the number L3039, stamped two times on the spar and poorly applied in both cases.

The starboard wing carries the number R33313, also stamped twice. This number differs in several ways to that of the port wing. Firstly, it is a

A close-up of part numbers on KD431's port and starboard wing spars. These numbers have been altered, and carry other inconsistencies that do not tally with the expected numbering sequence on these components. *(FAAM)*

five-digit number. One of the number sequences has the third digit (3) stamped first as a 5 and then overstamped by a 3. The resulting mess is not clearly defined, and one wonders if the restamped number was an attempt to clarify this. However, this would not explain why the port wing is stamped twice. The starboard wing number sequences also carry a single letter 'B', positioned midway between them.

As the wings carry Briggs plates stamped BRIT (to identify British-contract wings) this could refer to this specification. However, the port wing is devoid of such a marking. Some research has indicated that these wing numbers should have matched side-for-side on new aircraft leaving the factory, only the L and R prefixes being different. This clearly is not the case with KD431, and numerous matching witness marks and squadron markings that appear on both wings from various proven points in time negate the theory that one or both wings had been changed in service. This is another clear indication of production line haste and substitution.

Work on the wings revealed several key points of interest. Furthermore, it opened a whole new historical debate concerning this aircraft, and where it was destined during its service career. Three rare and significant markings were about to emerge after years of concealment.

Removal of 1963-applied paint on the wings progressed as the team divided from work on the fuselage. Almost immediately a strange, grainy finish began to appear as paint layers were removed from around the engine air intake in the wing leading edge. This gave the impression that a sticky tape (or similar) had been applied as a strip around the intake mouth and then removed, leaving the residue gum and cloth imprint of the tape itself. Work on the lower fuselage panels near the wing root and surrounding the exhaust pipes revealed similar residue markings in the newly exposed paintwork below the 1963 layer. As more became exposed it seemed to follow a line similar to that of the areas protected during Class II storage procedure. This procedure ensured that all of the sensitive areas and exposed apertures on the aircraft (particularly exhaust pipes, air intakes and gun ports) were protected from ingress of water and foreign objects during long-term storage or transportation. The method used was to affix a piece of fabric, similar to wing-repair linen cloth, across the area to be protected, and secure it in position with a light coat of dope (a type of varnish, varying in strength, that would stick, tauten and waterproof the fabric). This temporary stiffened shield would then be removed, often simply by peeling and tearing, to uncover the protected areas of the delivered aircraft, ready for service. Many aircraft being delivered from America by sea, as exposed deck cargo, would have undergone this type of treatment to protect vulnerable areas from salt-water ingress. If this was the case, we could well have uncovered another rare (possibly unique) detail surviving on this aeroplane. As work progressed to the wing-fold area, yet more tape-line markings were revealed along the wing-fold line of both the inner and outer wing sections. This seemed to confirm that

Just dirty marks, or witness marks and evidence from the past? The wing-fold areas, exhaust pipes and engine air intakes of KD431 still carry the tape-line residue marks from the protective layer applied to these sensitive areas when the aircraft was shipped across the Atlantic in November 1944. Underwing details, such as stencils and spent-ammunition-chute cover strip tear-offs, are also all original from the Second World War. *(FAAM)*

the markings were indeed the residue marks from a previous storage treatment; but from what period?

As these tape-line markings were below the 1963 paint, the tape must have been applied before the aircraft arrived at Yeovilton. Cranfield College would not have needed to preserve the aircraft from the elements in this way, and photographs depicting aircraft at Cranfield show that it was not in storage-prepared condition while at the college. However, there is clear evidence of the tape-line markings on the aircraft in these photo-

graphs, putting the date of application before the Cranfield period. This leaves only two real possibilities:

1. The storage-protection layers were applied to the aircraft in 1946, when it left service, and were removed on its arrival at Cranfield.
2. The tape lines and residue marks dated from 1944, when the aircraft made its transatlantic journey to the UK as deck cargo.

Corsairs in storage on board the aircraft repair carrier HMS *Unicorn* in 1944 or 1945. The Class II storage technique of taping over sensitive areas such as wing folds and engine intakes is clearly seen. The tape and doped fabric residue in these areas on KD431 match this layout exactly. Note the Fairey Firefly Mk I in the background. *(FAAM)*

The first theory is not impossible but unlikely, as aircraft such as the Corsair were being struck off charge and scrapped at this time. There would have been little sense in applying this level of protection to an aircraft that would otherwise be reduced to scrap. Cranfield had no plans to fly the aircraft, intending only to use it as a wing-fold demonstration aircraft at the training college. This required only an auxiliary hydraulic supply, rather than running of the engine, so prevention of debris ingress into the engine would not have been essential.

The second theory seems more likely. Much documentary evidence exists showing this protective measure in use on Corsairs and other aircraft types being transported as open-deck cargo. On the photographs taken at Cranfield in the early 1950s the tape lines appear quite weathered and toned down, rather than 'freshly peeled'. Moreover, the aircraft was in service for only some eighteen months from when it made its sea crossing until its military life ended. Generally, it had not received the number of repaints and alterations that many longer-service aircraft might have undergone, and which could have removed these marks completely.

Either way, the storage preservative markings almost certainly dated from the 1940s, and added to the growing number of original, authentic and possibly unique features on this aircraft. Further evidence to suggest

Packed on the deck of HMS *Ravager*, brand new Goodyear Corsairs make the perilous Atlantic crossing to Britain. German U-boats posed the greatest threat; one well-aimed torpedo could dispense with a hundred or more aircraft being transported in this way. This picture is dated November 1944, so KD431 could well be in this shipment. *(FAAM)*

that they remained from its original delivery date came with the removal of the paintwork around the wing gun ports in the wing leading edge.

Removal of the 1963 blue paint finish revealed the faded reddish-brown colour of the fabric dope used to stick a protective strip across the muzzles of the internally mounted wing guns. This was common practice in service to prevent foreign objects, dirt, insects and water entering the barrels of the guns before use and causing a potential blockage. A factory-applied transfer (sticker or decal) is positioned immediately behind the gun muzzle ports, on the lower surface of both wings, and reads 'REMOVE TAPE BEFORE FIRING'. This obviously refers to any protective strips applied to the gun ports, as detailed above, as any obstruction across the barrel of a gun can cause momentary back-pressure that could damage the weapon. However, many photographs show Corsairs and other aircraft types taking off and in flight with their gun ports clearly still taped. While some of these pictures may well portray training flights with unloaded guns, others clearly depict combat-prepared aircraft within active combat zones.

One former Corsair pilot recalls that the danger of back-pressure damage was considered low by his squadron commander, and that the excess drag caused by the open gun-port apertures was believed to be more harmful, in terms of reduced airspeed and in-flight handling effects. This resulted, on his particular squadron, in all flights being made with the gun ports taped over for these specific reasons. (Considering that the small

Gun-port cover strips are often reproduced on rebuilt and repainted aircraft as neatly marked out, tape-covered areas. In reality these fabric strips were often just cut to the nearest inch, pasted on, and then ripped off as required. These remains of roughly applied gun-port cover strips on KD431 date from 1944–5. *(FAAM)*

KD431, looking war-worn and in its original state. The essence of the project was *not* to add modern materials or finishes. *(FAAM)*

wooden stall block attached to the starboard wing could achieve such critical effects in flight, this decision does indeed seem logical.)

The same wording has been stencil-applied 24in behind this factory-applied sticker, using red paint. This appears to be an in-service addition to the factory warning instruction, and refers to the apertures from which the spent ammunition cartridges were ejected after firing. Similarly, these would have been taped over when the aircraft was parked for any length of time, again to prevent the ingress of debris that might cause the ejected cartridges to jam in the exit chutes. Spent and ejected ammunition cases, however, would not break through the tapes, so it would have been essential to remove these tapes before activating the guns.

Repeated gun servicing and subsequent replacing of these protective patches had resulted in a build-up of several layers of the dope varnish in this area of the wing. The area that the dope/varnish covered had now broadened to cover a portion of the wing in the same area as the Class II storage preservative tape lines. Careful removal of a small area of the varnish revealed what we had all hoped to find. The stage II preservative-tape lines continued underneath the service-applied red/brown varnish.

These wings were as original as we could hope to find. They still had factory-applied paint and stencils, and now the residue of the deck cargo treatment from November 1944 emphasised just how relatively unaltered this aircraft was.

The Cranfield photographs also show quite clearly some light-coloured markings on the outboard edges of the wing stubs, just at the point of the wing fold. Work on this area of the wing revealed areas of bright yellow paint, concealed below the 1963 blue paint finish. First thoughts were that this might be a service-applied recognition marking, possibly applied immediately postwar while the aircraft was with 768 Sqn. However, further exposure of the yellow areas showed that the markings had been very crudely applied; daubed rather than uniformly painted. Corresponding areas on the flaps, and also a splash of yellow applied to the outermost point of the wing-fold brackets, seemed to indicate a more likely reason for these hand-applied highlights.

This aircraft, along with numerous others awaiting scrapping and disposal, had been kept at RNAY Donibristle in Scotland immediately before its release to Cranfield in May 1946. It had obviously made its way over 400 miles south to Cranfield, but how? There were no reliable references to it having been flown there, so transportation by road seemed to be the only logical alternative. The aircraft would almost certainly have been trailered behind a suitable lorry, though the possibility that it was towed backwards by a lorry, on its own undercarriage, cannot be ruled out. This method of moving aircraft on public roads is not unknown, but not normally over such distances. Either way, the outermost points and protrusions would have needed to be highlighted for the safety of other road users, and I am sure that this explains the yellow-painted areas. Fortunately this yellow paint had not adhered well to the original blue finish that we wished to preserve as part of the original finish.

The outer wings on all British and other early Corsairs were linen fabric covered over metal-framed wing panels. This satisfied several needs during manufacture, and also facilitated repair in the field. Wings covered with

Discovered during paint removal, these yellow markings on the wing-root extremities are collision hazard markings applied for KD431's long road journey south from Donibristle to Cranfield. This journey of more than 400 miles on pre-motorway roads must have seen KD431 squeeze through many towns and villages. The yellow markings are clearly visible on a number of photographs of the aircraft taken at Cranfield during 1946–63. *(FAAM)*

Corsair KD431's outer wing panel uncovered and ready to receive a replacement fabric skin. The new starboard wing covering was copied from that of the factory-original port wing almost to the stitch.
(J. Coombes)

cotton fabric, shrunk and tautened into place, were significantly lighter than those skinned with aluminium sheet. There was also the consideration of cost saving compared with the use of aluminium during the war, and skilled sheet-metal workers were not required if a job could be designed to use an alternative material. The wing covering on the starboard side of the aircraft was poorly applied and beginning to detach itself from the wing framework. The photographs from Cranfield clearly show that this fabric had been removed at the college to allow the students to view the wing-folding mechanism as part of their studies. This was verified by two former Cranfield College lecturers. Research had also put me in contact with an ex- Royal Navy engineer, who recalled that, as an apprentice navy fitter, stationed at Yeovilton in 1963, he had volunteered (with others) to re-cover the exposed wing panel to make the aircraft look more complete. This fabric covering had apparently been applied with limited resources, and was intended to serve as a tidying-up job, rather than a determined effort to replicate the factory-applied fabric work.

In the light of this knowledge it was decided to remove the fabric completely from this wing and replace it with new material. This time, however, we would use the factory-original port wing as an exact template to copy. American linen fabric of the correct grade and specification was sourced to ensure the closest possible match to the original material. The entire port wing was then studied in detail to provide the mirror-image pattern for the starboard wing. During the re-covering of the wing, great trouble was taken to ensure that the fabric strips and taped seams, and the angles of cuts and overlaps, accurately matched those of the factory-original port side. In places even the number of stitches was counted, and an optical borescope was used on the port wing to provide an accurate understanding of certain details, layers and folds hidden from view by the wing's outer fabric covering.

The wing fabric is fastened to the wing framework by long thin strips of aluminium. These strips are held in place by force-fit clips and very small bolts and captive nuts that sandwich the fabric to the wing ribs. This method of fixing requires a specially constructed wing-rib section (to allow for the clips and bolts), but does save a lot of time-consuming labour that would otherwise be required to stitch the fabric to the frames with cotton thread.

While examining the inside of the port (factory-original) wing, it was noticed that the exposed threaded tip portion of the small bolts used to

With the new fabric covering in place, it was decided to refinish the panel with only an accurate colour-match blue, leaving the markings and stencilling incomplete. The aim of the project was to uncover the original 1944/5 finish, keeping twenty-first-century additions to an absolute minimum. *(FAAM)*

hold the fabric strips in place were primer coated. This was not unusual in itself, but it was noticed that the remaining threaded portion of the bolts was not primer coated. This indicated that the bolt tips and captive nuts on the inside of the wing had received a primer paint treatment after fitting. However, this would have been on the now-enclosed side of the wing, and there were no traces of paint splashes or overspray residues on any of the adjacent internal fabric surfaces. Until accurate information becomes available, this assembly sequence remains a complete mystery.

One interesting feature that survives as an original factory fitment to the starboard wing is the leading-edge stall block. This small wooden stream-lined block, 7in long by 3in wide by 2in high, is attached to the wing leading edge 115in in from the wingtip. The purpose of this simple device was to disturb the airflow across the starboard wing during the slow-speed approach to landing, and cause the wing to stall (lose lift) at the same rate (or just ahead of) the port wing. Thus the aircraft is much easier to control on a slow left-hand banked turn, with less chance of one wing losing lift (port side) while the other (starboard side) is still generating lift, causing a potentially unrecoverable stall. This was also important when the enormous torque effect of the revolving propeller was brought into consideration. Early marks of Corsair were not fitted with stall blocks, and many later aircraft were rebuilt with modified or non-original stall blocks. That fitted to KD431 is completely original, and may well be the last unaltered example to be found on a Corsair. Beneath the fabric covering and dark blue paint of the stall block the paint finish is mid-blue, in accordance with the US Navy three-tone colour scheme. This strongly suggests that KD431's stall block is a factory-fitted item that was painted (in this area of the wing only) in the US Navy mid-blue colour. It is not known whether the block was pre-finished in this colour before fitting, or this small area of wing was painted mid-blue after the block had been fitted.

A close-up of the starboard wing leading-edge stall block. This was often thought to be a post-factory modification on Corsairs, but the US Navy mid-blue paint on and around this component clearly indicates that it was a factory-fitted item. *(FAAM)*

The outer wings are of the cropped type, as previously mentioned, being 8in shorter than the wings fitted to US Navy Corsairs. This modification was necessary to enable the aircraft to fit within the 17ft 6in headroom limitation of British aircraft carriers. It was approved and carried out by the manufacturer, and became standard for all British-contract Corsairs. There is also some belief that the shorter-span wing improved the Corsair's flying characteristics in a roll manoeuvre, but this remains unconfirmed.

In the outer wing section of each wing there is an internal fuel tank. This was fitted to meet a requirement for British Corsairs, and remained a specified item for the duration of Corsair supply to the FAA. The fuel tank filler caps of KD431 had been overpainted in bright red gloss enamel paint in 1963. Careful removal of this paint, using a scalpel, revealed the original matt red finish, and also the factory-applied lettering stating the tank capacity of 47½ gallons.

During removal of the paint layer on the wings it proved possible to uncover and preserve many (possibly the entire wing set) of the ink-block-applied stencils indicating earthing points, areas to hold or step upon safely (or not, as directed), access panels and so on, as applied by the

Packed like sardines, these Corsairs below deck on HMS *Illustrious* in the East Indies provide a superb illustration of how vital it was to reduce the wingspan of British Corsairs to enable them to fit within the available hangar headroom when their wings were folded. Note the variations in Far Eastern roundel markings on some aircraft, before the introduction of full British Pacific Fleet markings. Individual crews' interpretations of the specification and instructions clearly varied. *(FAAM)*

A sequence of images taken from directly overhead, showing the original paint, wear marks and details exposed during the restoration. Nothing is faked, copied or mimicked; what you see is 100 per cent 1944/5. *(FAAM)*

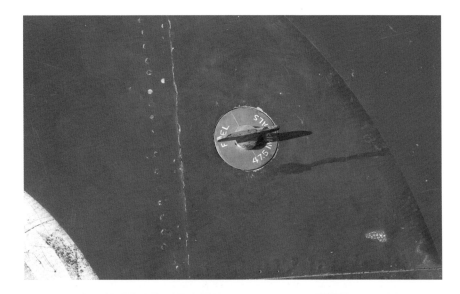

A close-up of the wing fuel tank filler cap. Authentic Second World War paintwork is a rare find, often having been lost through abrasive or chemical stripping processes. The painstaking approach adopted on this project produced such results time after time. *(FAAM)*

As with the fuselage stencils, the factory-applied wing stencils on KD431 were found to have been applied twice. *(FAAM)*

factory. Many of these original markings are again stamped twice, sometimes making the wording difficult to understand, as we had found on the nose portion of the fuselage.

At the root end of the outer wing section, positioned so as to be clearly visible with the wings in the raised and folded position, is a large transfer or sticker warning against working on the aircraft with the wings folded and not securely supported by a safety bar or jury strut. These transfers, too, had been overpainted, but careful paint removal has revealed these rare items and left them intact. Surprisingly, they have a bright, slightly reflective finish, unlike anything else on the aircraft's exterior.

The message they relay is repeated on similar transfers affixed to the exposed end of the inner wing stub. These wing-stub information transfers use the same colours, layout and wording as those on the outer wing, but the transfers have more of a matt tone finish. They appear to have been

Original warning transfers on the wings (and on some other areas) used a slightly reflective-finish, foil-type transfer. Note again the remains of the wing-fold preservative tape line, and other original factory markings. *(FAAM)*

coated with a semi-clear or brownish film or varnish. It was a surprise to see slightly reflective films and transfers being used in the 1940s, when one considers these to be a more modern invention.

The main and most obvious markings on the wings are the British insignia roundels. Variations of this type of identification marking, comprising red, white and blue concentric rings marked on both the upper and lower surfaces of an aircraft's wings, have been used on British military aircraft since the First World War. Today, the size of the rings and combination of the three colours varies according to Ministry of Defence specifications and orders. Then as now, these criteria can be determined by such conditions as the colour scheme of the aircraft or a particular theatre of war, and can be altered (in accordance with official instructions) at any given time. During the Second World War this became further complicated as the war in Europe drew to a close and the war in the East developed.

Corsair KD431 was delivered from the factory with Type C roundels applied to the lower wing surfaces. This type of roundel had a 32in-diameter blue outer circle and a 12in-diameter red central circle, separated by a 2in-wide thin white ring (making this portion, in effect, a ring of 16in in diameter). This was the correct specification of marking for the under-side of British naval aircraft at that time.

The upper wing surfaces originally carried the Type B roundel, consisting of just a red central circle surrounded by a larger blue circle, with no intermediate white ring. The officially specified sizes for this type of roundel required the central (red) circle to be two-thirds the total diameter of the outer (blue) circle. Typically, this roundel was applied to upper wing surfaces only, and therefore the standard blue-circle diameter of 60in was normally used. However, accurate measurement of the original remaining roundel on KD431 showed that even factory applied markings did not always follow such instructions. The diameter of the outer blue circle is 59½in, a little under the specified 60in, which should have made the inner red circle 20in. The actual measurement of the red portion is 24in. This may seem like splitting hairs, but it proves that inconsistencies and inaccuracies occurred even at factory level, despite explicit instructions. It would be interesting to know if this difference was the result of poor marking-out and application or, perhaps, the convenience of a readily available template to a nominal size. Whatever the case, this clearly demonstrates the pitfalls of textbook statements, often from very official sources, compared with the object itself.

Closer inspection of this upper surface roundel also showed that the original inner red circle was applied with a diameter of 30in. This being the first application of colour, it was then overlapped by 3in when the blue of the outer circle was applied as the second part of the operation. Again, this might seem an insignificant detail, but it shows further inconsistencies with measurements, and also the order of application.

During the aircraft's Service life these upper-surface roundels were modified to include a white separation band, applied between the red and blue circles.

By the spring of 1945 the Type B upper-surface roundels on British aircraft would have undergone modification in the field, having a white band added that clearly defined their red and blue portions. However, in the case of aircraft heading further east for combat against Japanese forces, further modifications were necessary. The Japanese national insignia was a red circle, often with a thin white outer band, and there was a very real danger of misidentification in aerial combat, where split-second decisions had to be made. British aircraft destined for this theatre underwent a further roundel modification, once outside British waters, to

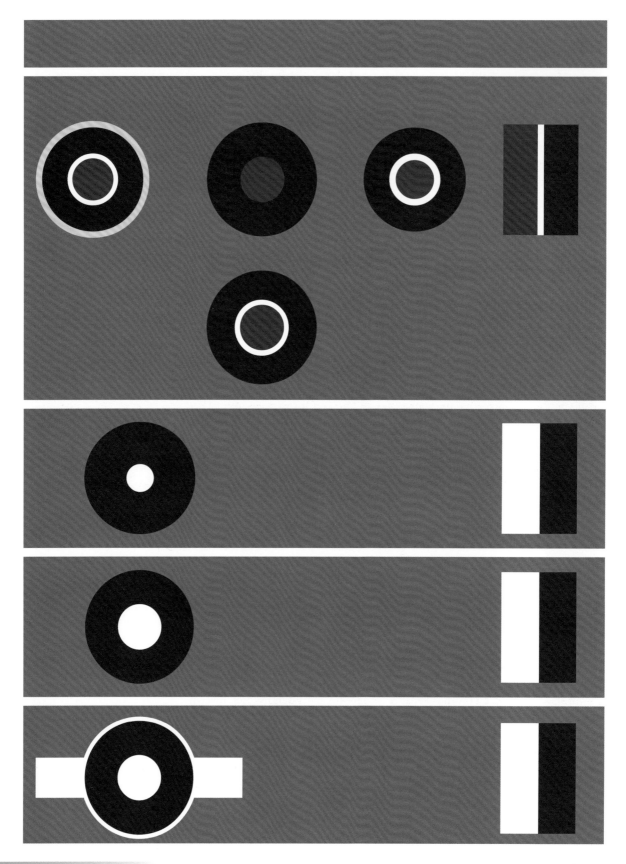

remove all red areas of the national insignia. The instruction would have been an officially dated signal from the Admiralty, distributed to all operational units, aircraft repair stations and air yards. However, individual interpretations of the signal by different squadron senior officers or aircraft maintainers (and also lack of available materials under wartime conditions), produced a variety of results that differed from the official specification.

The East Indies Fleet (including a force of British aircraft carriers operating in support of the Fourteenth Army in Ceylon, India and on the Burma coast) had already adopted a scheme with no red portion to the insignia on its aircraft. The central circles of the roundels, now white, were also reduced in size.

South East Asia Command, operating in support of Mountbatten's command strategies in Singapore, had its own variation of markings. Red was eliminated from the national insignia, all-blue roundels with white circular centres being applied to the wings and fuselage sides. The white centres were intended to be one-quarter the diameter of the overall roundel, but they often varied widely with individual interpretation and applications. The fin insignia was to be altered to one blue and one white stripe, instead of red, white and blue, with the white stripe leading.

The British Pacific Fleet operated under the strategic direction of Adm Chester Nimitz, Commander-in-Chief Pacific Ocean areas. It fought alongside the US Fifth and Third Pacific Fleets off the coast of Japan and its islands. At this point the FAA adopted an insignia incorporating a roundel and bar, more closely matching the US star and bar. Some of the aircraft would have been modified and delivered from aircraft yards that had reasonable painting facilities. Many would have been altered at sea by the individual squadrons, with limited facilities and in cramped hangar conditions.

No British aircraft are known to have been supplied from manufacturers with any of these versions of insignia factory applied. The results are numerous and variable and often fall outside the original specification.

The roundels on both wings of KD431 had been overpainted in 1963 with much brighter polyurethane high-gloss paint, in an attempt to enhance the 1944/5 markings for display purposes. Although this had been neatly done, the roundels were in completely incorrect colour tones. The 1944/5 roundels, which hopefully still existed beneath, would have used much more drab tones, with a matt finish. Removing polyurethane paint (best described as coloured glue) from on top of thin cellulose paint applied some sixty years ago provided a very new challenge. A small test area was marked out to see if this was possible, and various trials were conducted. Our own acquired knowledge of paint-removing techniques led us to experiment with sliding a fine scalpel blade between the two paint layers and lifting one away

Opposite: The basic specification for standard national markings as applied to British naval aircraft in 1942/7, and examples of intended alterations for FAA aircraft operating over Far Eastern waters.

Standard Type C1 roundel. Applied to fuselage side (typically 54in overall diameter, or proportional to fuselage side). Red, white and blue, with dull yellow 2in outer band.

Standard Type B roundel. Upper surfaces. Red and blue (no white band); red portion to be one-third the diameter of the total roundel diameter. (Existing Type B roundels were modified at squadron level from January 1945 by the application of a white band.)

Standard Type C roundel. Applied to upper and lower surfaces (typically of smaller overall dimensions on lower surfaces).

Standard fin flash. Red and blue, separated equally by 2in-wide white band. Red portion leading.

East Indies Fleet. Roundels – red colouring to be replaced by white. Remainder of roundel to show as blue only. Fin flash to be modified to replace red colouring with white (white portion leading).

South East Asia Command. Roundels – red to be eliminated from national marking. Roundel to consist of blue ring with white circular centre. Fin flash to be modified to replace red colouring with white (white portion leading).

British Pacific Fleet. Roundels – national marking to consist of blue ring with narrow white border and a white circular centre. On either side of the roundel there were white rectangular panels, similar to those used in the United States' insignia. Fin flash to be modified to replace red colour with white (white portion leading). *(FAAM)*

from the other. This demanded extreme concentration, patience, and a
steady hand, and only very small areas could be removed at a time.
Bearing in mind that the area of the roundels was nearly 3,000sq in, this
was a daunting task indeed, but one that the team thought worthwhile if
the desired result could be achieved.

The work rate was slow, and remained slow even as abilities and
confidence levels rose. But the outcome justified all of the laborious effort
and frustration. Here again we were uncovering actual 1940s paint,
showing the roundels in their correct colours. These were not similar
colours, or a close match. It was the actual paint applied in 1944. This
was possibly the last known set of truly authentic and original roundels
surviving from the Second World War. Our meticulous paint-layer removal
and study of the roundels during this process also provided a fascinating
insight into wartime Service methodology regarding markings details
and changes.

The first point of interest was that the blue paint used for the outer ring
of the roundel differed very little from the wing colour itself. As we know,
this paintwork was applied on the Goodyear assembly line, in the USA,

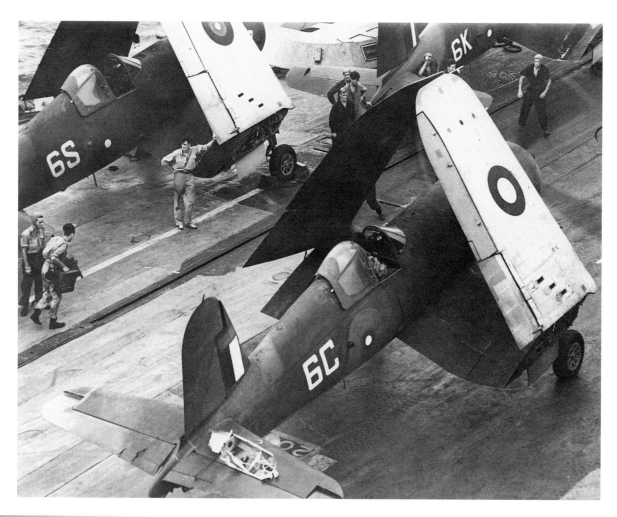

and Corsairs were also being finished to US Navy specification in the same factory at the same time. The 'star and bar' national insignia, applied as part of the USA's own aircraft colour schemes, used a darker blue background (behind the star emblem) than the blue used as the outer band on normal British roundels. One theory is that Goodyear used the same blue for both US and British roundel backgrounds; hence the similarity with the wing colour. Here again, lack of official factory information leaves this question unresolved.

The next fascinating discovery was that white rings had been applied to the upper-wing-surface roundels. Research had confirmed that all new Corsairs delivered at the time KD431 was built would not have had white rings on their upper-surface roundels. A closer study of this newly exposed area also showed that the white rings were applied in a less uniform and neat fashion than the original red and blue background rings. We were looking at an in-Service modification to the roundels, carried out at unit level. As mentioned earlier, this modification arose from a March 1945 requirement to enhance identification of British aircraft when viewed from above. Initially used in the closing stages of the European theatre, it was

Removal of the upper-wing-surface roundel paint. It was exciting to break through the 1963 polyurethane gloss paint and discover that the original 1940s subdued finish markings still existed. *(FAAM)*

Using a scalpel blade to pick and peel away at the modern paint, fractions of an inch at a time, was often the only effective way to separate the new and old layers of paint. This partly exposed roundel represents 40–50 hours of painstaking, delicate work. *(FAAM)*

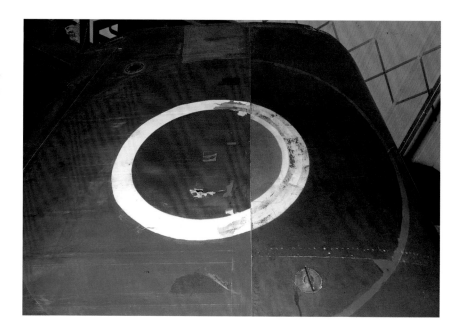

carried over for identification purposes in the Pacific, being superseded by a revised roundel-and-bar insignia to coincide with the American national insignia. This once-common Second World War alteration is now another possibly unique detail preserved on this time-capsule aircraft.

The white rings themselves, approximately 4in wide, appear to have undergone a sequence of applications, which gives a valuable insight into the application techniques (and possibly the thought processes) of an FAA squadron at the time.

It appears that a freehand attempt to apply the white rings was made initially, using a 1in paint brush. The inside and outside diameters had been defined in this way, with at least one in-fill ring applied. However, the white bands were not completed using this technique, and the edges lack neatness. At the centre of the roundel (on the port wing) a small fabric patch 2in square had been stuck into position, adhered by dope and painted over in a matt red paint to match the surrounding roundel colour. One edge of this patch had become sufficiently detached to allow a view beneath. The patch appears to be covering a pierce in the wing fabric, at the exact centre point of the roundel. It seems that this patch repair covers the hole made by the use of a pin-and-string form of 'compass' that might have been used to scribe the white band outlines before painting. (The starboard wing fabric, having been replaced in 1963, has lost any such witness mark). This method then appears to have been abandoned in favour of another technique.

A second application, over the top of the brush-painted rings, gave the appearance of a stippled finish, not dissimilar to that produced by a small paint roller, approximately 4in wide. Overlapping parallel lines, spanning the width of the white rings and appearing to be stop and re-start points similar to those left during paint-roller use, were evident at various stages

around the white ring. Was a paint roller really the solution to this problem? Although this initially seemed to be so, it was necessary to confirm whether this now-common tool was readily or widely available in 1945. Closer inspection with a magnifying glass showed the stippled effect to be that of a spray-painting technique.

This closer study also yielded a conclusive and fascinating detail. The white ring applied to the starboard wing, put on following the sequence described above, shows an imperfection in the paint on its inside diameter that is not readily visible at first observation. Following the inside diameter line around, an exact repeat of the imperfection recurs 18in away from the first. The overlap lines spanning the width of the white ring were now also noticed to be at equal distances from the repeated imperfections. It all seemed to make sense. A curved masking template approximately 18in long had been made, perhaps from paper or card, and progressively moved around the roundel, providing the stencil to spray the required white ring. The repeated imperfection was an irregularity in the edge of the masking template.

This level of scrutiny and deduction might seem rather extreme, but it is essential if one is to understand *exactly* what has happened to an object, an aircraft in this case, during each stage of its existence. More importantly, it provides an accurate insight into how these changes

With the brush-painted concentric white-band technique abandoned, the application method changed to spray painting, using a curved mask that was repeatedly repositioned to produce a complete circle. *(FAAM)*

were made and exactly how people carried out the work. But why was our discovery so important or remarkable?

It is widely known that markings such as these were applied and modified during an aircraft's Service life, but a mere sixty years later virtually all original Second World War examples have been lost, having been removed during progressive in-service modifications or, subsequently, by countless innocent but historically destructive 'restorations'. Furthermore, few people seem to be able to recall with any accuracy how this work was *really* thought through and carried out at the time. The same old generalisations seem to prevail: 'They would have just painted them on by hand', or similar remarks. Yet aircraft restorers, historians, model makers, artists and authors often debate at length the details of how such markings were applied, where on the aircraft they were positioned, how neatly they would have been applied, what is and is not correct, and so on. All of this is now important to them, but few, if any, true examples remain to provide conclusive evidence for these various debates.

Here again was the difference and the proof. Here we could see how a particular process was really carried out on one particular squadron, at one point in time. This ordinary task had been achieved by a development of techniques and thoughts. In 1945 there were no superstores selling endless quantities of masking tape. There were no huge pieces of cardboard, today so commonly left over from a consumer product packaging, from which to cut a whole circular stencil. Whether the change of

technique was dictated by speed of application, neatness, or other factors, may yet still be discovered. What is more important is that we have one of the last examples, if not the last example, of such markings, and one of the last chances to preserve and record them and gain an accurate understanding of how they were applied.

CONTROL SURFACES

The control surfaces on the wing trailing edges also revealed several points of interest when thoroughly examined. One was that the ailerons were found to be made from wood. A combination of weight, balance and profile was critical to the effective operation of the ailerons. After extensive trials, plywood construction was found to be preferable to aluminium for these components. The result was control surfaces that could produce a 180-degree roll rate in one second. These outer wing control surfaces are marked with an anchor symbol and US Navy ink stamp on the first inner rib, visible through a small access hole. Similarly, the inboard flaps have traces of the US Navy three-tone colour scheme showing through beneath the factory-applied dark glossy blue paint finish. This is further evidence of contract-supplied components being delivered or pre-prepared to a US Navy specification paint scheme, but being factory-fitted to British-contract aircraft and resprayed accordingly.

Few aircraft exist today with such extensive and complete Second World War markings as found on KD431. Each preserved area and detail provides valuable, exacting and, in places, unique references to colours, positioning, materials and techniques used. Note the green paint showing through on the outer-wing ammunition tank. *(FAAM)*

The port aileron removed for examination and cleaning. Critical weight, balance and profile combinations of this component were found to be more easily achieved with wood than with metal. An internal examination through the small access hole showed that this component was drawn from a stock of parts built to US Navy specification. *(FAAM)*

GUN BAYS

The main fixed armament for the Corsair consisted of six 0.50in Browning machine guns, three being fitted internally into each wing. These guns, manufactured by the Colt Patent Firearms Company, provided the Corsair with extremely heavy firepower, greater than that of many fighters of the time, and helped the Corsair earn its reputation as a formidable combat aircraft.

The guns had been removed from KD431, probably at Donibristle, Scotland, in 1946, when the aircraft was selected to go to the College of Aeronautics at Cranfield.

The ammunition containers (tanks) and belt feeds remain intact and appear to be a complete set as originally fitted. The tanks are made from aluminium, spray-painted with primer on the surfaces normally concealed within the wing, and the lids of the tanks are finished to match the exterior wing finish, in this case dark blue. However, careful examination and paint removal on the lids of the tanks revealed that two of the tanks had an olive green paint finish applied directly beneath that of the Goodyear factory-applied dark blue. This immediately prompted a more thorough examination of the tank set, and a thought process as to how

The ammunition tanks fitted to KD431 are a complete set, and in very good condition. Note that the lid of this tank has been sprayed olive green beneath the Goodyear factory-applied glossy sea blue finish. *(FAAM)*

this might have come to be. The only temperate-camouflaged Corsairs were built by Vought or Brewster (the significance of this appeared later in the project).

Access for servicing and arming the guns and removing the ammunition tanks is via hinged panels on the upper surface of the wings. Removal of the tank set for more thorough cleaning (after careful labelling regarding their position in the aircraft) also allowed a full examination and comparison of details and witness marks between all the tanks.

The first point of note was that they were all in good condition. The primer finish and foil instruction transfers (decals) showed very little wear or damage on both the inner and outer faces of all the tanks. (It was also noteworthy that bright semi-reflective foil stickers had again been used.) Various handwritten numbers had been applied to the primer surfaces of the tanks using pencil and coloured crayon. These appeared to be factory-part or batch numbering, and although the writing style and numbering was similar, there was no obvious sequence or link between these hand-applied references. On the outer surface of the tank lids (on top of the blue factory-applied paint finish) a single number had been very neatly applied (freehand by brush) in black paint, using the central rivet of the tank as a reference point in each case. The brush application suggests a post-factory application. The numbering, its style, and application suggests that it was done by the same person on all of the ammunition tanks. No other numbers have been applied on previous or subsequent paint layers, including the two tanks that have the olive green finish beneath the dark blue.

During operational use, the moving ammunition inevitably wore some of the primer finish away from the tanks' inside surfaces. This was caused as the cannon shells were pulled, on their continuous belts, out of the tanks and fed into the gun's mechanism for firing. The thin outside primer finish also accumulated wear marks, scratches and the like as a direct result of being pulled out of and reinserted into their respective wing compartments during ammunition replenishment. The lack of wear on all of the tanks

Opposite: The 0.50in machine guns were removed from KD431 before it was released from the Royal Navy. However, the remainder of the gun bays and the ammunition-belt feed tracks are intact and extremely complete. The phrase 'giving it the whole nine yards' is alleged to have an association with the Corsair, 'nine yards' supposedly being the approximate total length of the belted ammunition carried by the aircraft. Even if this is not true, it well describes the firepower that could be delivered from this awesome gun platform. (FAAM)

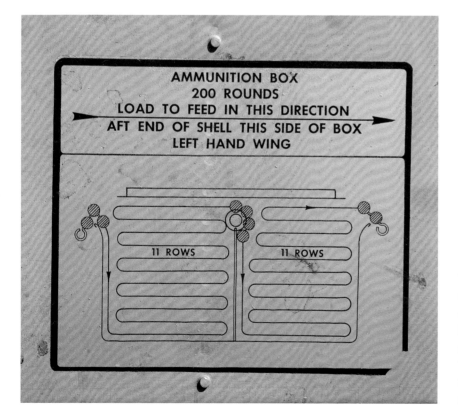

AMMUNITION BOX
200 ROUNDS
LOAD TO FEED IN THIS DIRECTION
AFT END OF SHELL THIS SIDE OF BOX
LEFT HAND WING

11 ROWS   11 ROWS

The original instruction transfers on the ammunition tanks are in extremely good condition, having been concealed from light and untouched for so many years. These transfers are also made from a slightly reflective foil-like material. (FAAM)

corresponds with the fact that the aircraft spent only a short time in service, and was not engaged in active combat. It has been confirmed that the guns were fired during training activities carried out by 1835 Sqn in Northern Ireland, but extensive use does not seem to have taken place.

The green paint applied to the two tank lids (beneath the Goodyear factory blue finish) was spray-applied, and gives every indication of also being a factory or professionally applied finish. The colour is correct for temperate camouflage paint schemes applied to the upper surfaces of British military aircraft, but should not appear on a Goodyear-built Corsair for one very simple reason: green-camouflaged Corsairs were not produced by the Goodyear factory. Similarly, Brewster did not produce all dark blue Corsairs, so another riddle concerning KD431 arises.

Earlier Corsairs produced by Brewster were finished in temperate camouflage; green and slate-grey upper surfaces with sky ('duck egg') lower surfaces, but production of these ceased in June 1944 with the enforced closure of the Brewster factory. All Corsairs supplied to the FAA from the Goodyear production lines were finished in all over dark blue, KD431's main finish.

One other area, on the tail of the aircraft, had also revealed evidence of green camouflage paint, discovered during a close inspection of the aircraft before work began. Although this had yet to be fully investigated, it was possible that, at some stage, KD431 was fitted with parts from (or destined for) a Brewster-built Corsair. Determining accurately at what stage these might have been fitted could add a new dimension to the aircraft's history. It would have been easy to assume that the ammunition tanks were swapped at some stage (while the aircraft was with 1835 or 768 Sqn) with two tanks from an earlier Brewster-built Corsair Mk III, several of which were certainly being flown on these squadrons at that time. However, when we theorised and examined the paint and marking applications in sequence this became a flawed assumption, for several reasons:

- The black numbers are applied to the factory blue paint and all match perfectly.

- The numbers on the tanks that have green paint beneath the blue have not been reapplied or added over previous numbers.

- The handwritten pencil and crayon references on the primer surfaces all appear to match in style and application on all tanks, though their numerical sequence does not match.

- Switching green tanks on to a blue aircraft is a fairly obvious error, unlikely to have been easily made or to have gone unnoticed for long.

- If the tanks had been swapped in service with two from a Brewster aircraft, why were they spray-painted blue? Had they been refitted to the original aircraft, the colour would also not have matched. Moreover, the black numbering (or sequence) might not have matched had they been refitted to the Brewster aircraft.

○   The blue finish appears to be a factory application, not an in-service modification.

○   The wear on the inside and outside of the tanks seems consistent throughout the set, not being excessive or different on the two green-painted tanks. This, too, is strange, as the green tanks would have been in service longer had they come from an earlier, Brewster Corsair Mk III.

○   Ammunition tank removal, replenishment and replacement discipline would not normally permit such a potentially serious error. Although not impossible, in-service, swapping between Goodyear aircraft would probably have been frowned upon, and swapping between Brewster and Goodyear marks even more so. In an active combat zone with limited resources this might well have been permissible, but on a training squadron such a practice would have been less common (or necessary).

If these components were fitted or swapped in service, any connection with the Brewster company would stop there. However, if they were fitted at the Goodyear factory they might well indicate a link with the closure of the Brewster factory, and components being transferred to Goodyear for use in its Corsair production. This likelihood is currently not clearly understood, and appears not to have been previously recorded.

WING-FOLD AREA

With the aircraft's wings folded, the wing-root ends, containing many of the mechanical actuating devices, are exposed. In this area there are numerous examples of components unaltered since factory production. Many of the hydraulic cylinders, connections and mechanical components fitted to the aircraft were from production stock, pre-finished in US Navy scheme mid-blue. When the aircraft received its overall dark blue finish, after final assembly, these components were painted in dark blue on their exposed side but retained the mid-blue on their shielded faces. All of these wing-folding components have clearly been on the aircraft since their original fitting and the final painting process, as can be deduced from studying the corresponding oversprayed and shielded areas surrounding each component. Similar oversprayed and unsprayed areas of aircraft framework and structure are also visible in the wing-fold area.

The aircraft appears to have had its final paint finish applied with the wings folded. This is revealed by an overspray line that runs the length of the inside face of the inner wing-stub section, an area that can only be accessed with the wings raised. This light coat of blue paint partly covers free-flowing handwritten pencil markings approximately 2in high that read R 85 on the port wing stub and R 8 231 on the starboard. These appear to be factory part numbers or fitting references, applied directly to the primer finish. If they are factory fitting references they appear to have been applied before the wings were fitted to the aircraft, as it is too

Overspray witness marks show that the aircraft was finish-sprayed in the Goodyear factory with its wings folded, and resprayed at Yeovilton in 1963 with the wings spread. Fortunately this preserved a large amount of original 1940s detail and reference information in the wing-fold areas. *(FAAM)*

Evidence that components were drawn from US Navy-specification stock and fitted to British-specification Corsairs. This hydraulic cylinder was originally finished in US Navy non-specular blue, and then, as the overspray witness marks show, partly coated with glossy sea blue after being fitted to KD431. Numerous components in the wing-fold and undercarriage bay areas show this telltale sign. *(FAAM)*

difficult, if not impossible, to access the area and hold a pencil to write clearly. This was a further tiny piece of evidence that helped to provide an overall picture of the sequence of the aircraft's construction.

Few of the hydraulic fittings are painted blue, though many are coloured blue by their anodised production finish. This is also correct and original from the factory. Painting the hydraulic fittings would not be regarded as good or standard practice, for fear that a small paint chip could enter and contaminate the fluid system when a pipe was disconnected and then replaced.

It appears that the 1963 respray of the aircraft was carried out with the wings unfolded, leaving the wing-fold areas essentially in their original factory condition.

INNER WING STUB AND CENTRE SECTION

The aircraft's arched centre section, incorporating the wing stubs and cockpit station, is the major component upon which the rest of the aircraft was built. It was the first portion to be set into a jig before rolling along the factory production line, growing stage by stage into a complete aircraft. Our detailed analysis of KD431 focused not only on what we could see, but also on trying to determine the exact date that it started its production-line journey. This would help to confirm what mark of Corsair KD431 really was.

One key feature that helps distinguish the FG-1A from FG-1D sub-types is the form of bomb-rack arrangement fitted to the underside of the centre

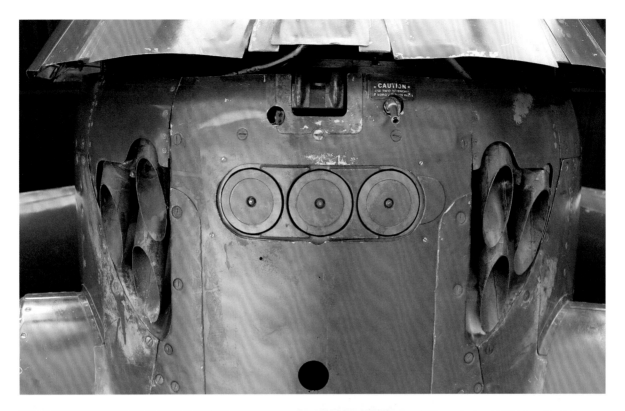

A view of the now very rare forward bomb-rail mounting bracket, situated below the engine compartment. This detail helps to distinguish a true FG-1A Corsair from an FG-1D type with underwing bomb mountings. This picture also shows to good effect the grouping and position of the exhaust pipes to make use of rearward thrust. Note also the residue tape marks around the exhaust area, remaining from the aircraft's transatlantic delivery in 1944, and the grey-painted inner surface of the cooling gills. *(FAAM)*

section. The FG-1A had only a single, centrally mounted bomb rail, using a forward-position hook-type lug mounted on the lower part of the engine mounting framework and a connection point mounted centrally under the belly of the centre section. One of the modifications that is always considered to be concurrent with the FG-1D is the provision of two extra underbelly bomb attachment points. These twin pylon mounts are a key structural part of the centre section, and would have been

The Corsair presented air fitters with the extra challenge of getting on to the aircraft's curved wing and staying there while carrying out essential servicing and repairs. The scratch marks and wear patterns seen here date from 1944/5, and demonstrate just how extensively the aircraft's surface could be damaged by repeated clambering, sliding and daily foot traffic. *(FAAM)*

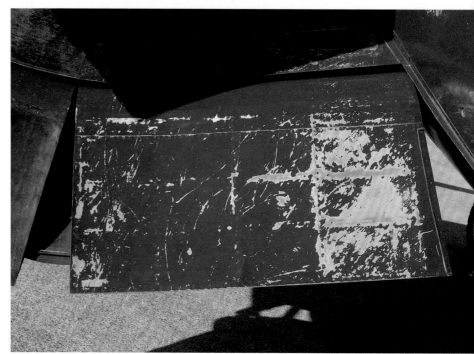

formed as a part of the initial centre-section structure. Corsair KD431 clearly has only the central bomb-rail attachment point, though unfortunately the rail is missing.

The inner, non-folding portions of the wings also revealed many interesting witness marks and features as the 1963 paint was removed. The curved, gull-wing shape of these wing stubs made the wing a very difficult area to climb up to and stand on. However, to enable the aircraft to be serviced, adjusted, armed and fuelled, such access was essential. Footsteps and slotted hand grips are provided at certain points to aid access to these areas, and white ink-block stencils indicate safe 'step' and 'hold' areas. Those areas where standing on, or holding part of the aircraft structure is not permitted are also marked. In theory, these instructions should have been followed religiously; in practice, however, the wear marks on the 1940s paintwork clearly shows that this was not always the case. Many areas of the wing display significant levels of paint erosion, and even deformed areas of the metal skin itself, owing to repeated clambering and stepping on to the wing.

How do we know the point in time from which these wear and witness marks originated?

- Research shows that, for almost all of the forty years that the aircraft has been on display within the FAAM, it has had its wings folded. (It was displayed with one wing down for a short period, but not for a significant length of time.)

- Work requiring access on the Corsair within the museum has been minimal, mostly being restricted to cleaning and dusting.

- With the wings in the folded position it is impossible to stand on or access the areas showing much of the erosion and wear.

- The erosion and wear marks are beneath the paint finish applied in 1963, and research shows that there have been no further paint applications since that time.

It is therefore logical to conclude that the wear marks were caused either at Cranfield College or earlier, in FAA service. While at Cranfield the aircraft would certainly have been accessed in some of the wear-mark areas, resulting in some proportion of the damage. However, as the aircraft was not started, flown, serviced, armed or refuelled while at the college, most of the witness marks must date from the aircraft's Second World War service.

GAS-REACTIVE PAINT PATCH

By far the most important discovery on the wing (and arguably during the whole project) was made in the area immediately inboard of the wing-fold joint on the upper surface of the port wing stub. While removing the 1963 paint in this location an unusual circular marking began to emerge. This handpainted marking, 10in in diameter, consisted of a dull yellow circle of 8in diameter surrounded by a red outer band approximately 1in wide. Both the yellow and red portions had been brush-painted, heavily applied, and appeared to have been applied freehand, with little or no marking-out.

Initially we were at a loss to understand this marking's purpose or appearance. Its size would have made it difficult to see at any distance, if it were an identification marking intended for use in flight. The colour scheme did not conform to any marking or insignia known to have been applied to FAA aircraft at that time. Initial thoughts centred on its use as a reference point or positioning point for an item of test equipment or apparatus used in association with studies at Cranfield College. However, it seemed too large, lacked accuracy of layout and its position made little sense as a measurement or reference point.

One theory, advanced by FAAM director Graham Mottram, was that the marking could have been related to similar markings used on Second World War aircraft in connection with gas- and chemical-agent recognition. Several weeks passed with no conclusion drawn, then a telephone conversation with Mr John Fricker, FRAeS regarding the loan of two Corsair photographs, added more substance and detail to this theory. I described the colour and position of the marking to Mr Fricker, who recognised it as being similar in colour to a particular marking applied to

Possibly the last Second World War gas-reactive paint patch left in existence. Concealed beneath a layer of paint for over forty years, it is a miracle that it has survived. Had KD431 been paint-stripped rather than investigated inch-by-inch, such details and markings would have been lost for ever. *(FAAM)*

some aircraft earlier in the war. This, however, was diamond-shaped rather than circular, and positioned on the upper part of the fuselage spine. If contaminated by certain gas vapour or chemicals it would change colour (from dull yellow to dull red), warning that the airfield had been subjected to an overnight enemy attack using a chemical or gas agent.

The theory was that any chemical agent dispersed from high altitude would descend on to an airfield and coat all exterior surfaces with a harmful chemical residue that, if touched, would cause severe blistering to hands and exposed skin. It was feared that this would render the whole airfield useless but capable of being captured intact by an invasion force. Similar markings were applied to easily visible areas such as the tops of pillar boxes, the petrol tanks and mudguards of motorcycles, the roofs of lorries and even purpose-made boards mounted like slanting bird tables.

For best effect the painted surface had to be exposed and facing the sky, but inclined at about 45 degrees so that the chemical agent would produce a more obvious, streaked appearance on contact. This method of early warning was also extended to civilian-populated areas near important target areas. All of this appeared to be fairly well documented with regard to the European theatre of war, and the then imminent threat of invasion of England from Germany. How though, did this correspond with the markings on KD431?

With the possibility of the paint being chemically reactive, it was necessary to establish if the paint itself could be in any way harmful to those working on it. It was arranged for a sample flake of the yellow paint to be analysed at Defence Science and Technologies Laboratories (DSTL) at Porton Down in Wiltshire. Hopefully, they would be able to confirm our theory and give best advice on the handling of the painted area. The result from DSTL was both conclusive and remarkable. Firstly, they confirmed that the paint was indeed a gas/chemical-reactive paint dating from the 1940s. They proved this by chemical analysis, and determined that the paint in question was known to them as paranitrophengeazobeta-naphthylamine. Further, they apparently carried out a very basic reaction test on the small sample provided, and reported that the paint changed colour. This was quite remarkable, bearing in mind that the paint was now nearly sixty years old.

This gave rise to a whole new series of questions. When exactly was it applied, by whom, where, and for what reason?

As already mentioned, it was known that diamond-shaped markings having a similar purpose were applied to aircraft in the earlier stages of the war, though no examples appear to have survived to enable a study or comparison. Knowing from our own research that KD431 was built in 1944, any thoughts of the gas patch being a remnant from an earlier period of the Second World War could be discounted. As the marking was on the fixed, inner wing stub it could not have been imported or substituted from another aircraft (if a wing change had taken place).

Study of our time-line diary for KD431 indicated that the aircraft had been attached to only two FAA squadrons. From January to August 1945 it appears to have been with 1835 Sqn, and from September to December

1945 it was attached to 768 Sqn. The aircraft's attachment to 768 Sqn was immediately postwar, and at second-line-squadron level. There seemed little need to apply a gas-reactive marker to the aircraft at this time. The marking was evidently hand-applied by brush, and gives the impression that it was not applied as a factory process. This suggests that it was applied either at one of the holding units on the aircraft's arrival in Great Britain (Aldergrove, Northern Ireland; RNAY Stretton, Cheshire) or while it was on 1835 Sqn.

Research shows that the Admiralty had in place at least two documents containing instructions relating to gas-reactive paint applications on FAA aircraft, dated 1939 and 1943 respectively. The first is a naval stores document (N.S. 0106/38 – 31.8.39) detailing application guidelines and instructions. It also specifies additional quantities of gas-reactive paint to be supplied to various RNAYs. The second document is a recording form (FONAS FORM 59), providing details of equipment and paint finishes and stating whether or not an aircraft is complete, airworthy and serviceable to fly. Provision for specifying if gas-reactive paint has been applied to an aircraft is made in item 3 on the form.

Few other references have been found concerning the use of gas-reactive paint on Royal Navy aircraft, particularly during the latter stages of the Second World War. The study of numerous archive photographs has, to date, yielded only one image that shows a marking that might be an

Positioned so as to be easily visible from the cockpit, the gas/chemical-reactive patch changed colour from dull yellow to reddish-brown if it was contaminated by deadly gas or chemical agents. *(FAAM)*

A war-worn Corsair wearing East Indies Fleet roundels comes to an unceremonious end in the carrier's crash barrier. This situation was bad enough in isolation but, if other aircraft were urgently waiting to land, deck crews had very little time to untangle a stricken aircraft and, if it was too badly damaged, push it over the side to clear the deck. The matching light-coloured diamond shapes on each wing might be gas-reactive paint patches, applied by someone more familiar with the earlier European war theatre positioning for such markings (diamond shapes applied with points trailing). Note that the aircraft has returned to the ship with its gun ports still taped over, the tape not having been removed before flight, and the guns evidently not having been fired. Four of the wing ammunition tanks have been replaced by units from a different-colour aircraft, and, more importantly with regard to the restoration team's researches, these have not been repainted to match the different paint scheme. *(FAAM)*

application of gas-reactive paint being used in the Eastern and Pacific theatre of war. This image shows a Corsair (coded 6X, believed to be an 1830 Sqn aircraft) during a deck-landing accident aboard an aircraft carrier, possibly HMS *Illustrious*. The aircraft is in East Indies Fleet markings, with the entire roundels painted over blue, with only small white centre spots. Positioned approximately centrally on each wing are two small diamond/square markings. These appear to be in a light matt finish and hand-applied. The gun ports are still covered with their doped fabric strips. If these were natural taupe-coloured fabric and dope, the colour tone would be similar to that of the pale ochre of gas-reactive paint. There is no normal reason to apply removable patches to this area of a Corsair wing. It would also be a great coincidence for damage repair patches to match side-for-side, in position, shape and size. If these are gas paint patches, the question also arises as to whether the person responsible for their application was familiar with the earlier wartime application specification of diamonds positioned relative to the aircraft's centreline? However, there is no conclusive evidence that these markings are gas-reactive patches. (Note also that the fuselage-side code number has been toned down from bright white, probably to pale blue or grey, and that four of the port wing ammunition tanks are dark in colour and might have been substituted from a dark blue aircraft. Moreover, the aircraft has just landed back on the ship and still has its wing gun ports taped over. Clearly they were not uncovered before flight.)

Gaining a better understanding of the reason for the gas patch on KD431 was proving harder than expected. Talking with the few remaining former 1835 Sqn pilots did produce one likely solution as to when and where the marking was applied, but no firm indication as to the exact destination of the squadron. Tony Mitchell, Stan Deeley, John Taylor, John Morton and former 1835 Sqn Senior Pilot Douglas Buchanan were all contacted as part of the research regarding KD431, and in particular its gas-detector patch. All had similar recollections of events at the time, and of the squadron's movements between January and August 1945.

Having finished their basic flying training in the USA and converted on to Corsairs, the pilots of 1835 Sqn redeployed to Eglinton in Northern Ireland to continue their fighter aircraft training. Initially this was undertaken on Brewster-built Corsair Mk IIIs, then later with the newly delivered Corsair Mk IVs, KD431 being one of the batch. This training consisted of deck-landing practice on HMS *Premier*, followed by ground-support training with various Army units. These training activities, co-ordinated by the Army and one RAF officer, were apparently rehearsals for proposed beach-landing offensives in the Far East, for which 1835 Sqn had been selected to provide support. They consisted of low-level attacks on disused vehicles (old buses and lorries positioned along the beach at Magillan Sands, Northern Ireland), using the aircraft's heavy-calibre machine-guns. Skip-bombing practice was also carried out on beachheads and small inlets along the coast. This technique required great skill to bring the aircraft in towards the chosen target (a ship, coastal cave, sheltered inlet or beach emplacement) and release a single bomb at the correct height. Approach speed and angle of dive was also critical, so that the released bomb would skip off the water (rather like bouncing a pebble across a lake) and into the target area. It was more accurate than high-altitude bomb dropping, and more effective if the target had to be struck from the side or within a covered area.

The intensive training took place from January to July 1945. This working-up period brought 1835 Sqn to a honed state of airmanship, proficient at deck-landing the Corsair, tight formation flying, combat manoeuvres and support cover for the Army if required.

The ultimate target that necessitated all this hard training was a closely guarded secret, and today the few surviving 1835 Sqn members can only guess as to their final destination. Some thought it was possibly in connection with the proposed Singapore offensive (to regain control of Singapore), but were never given an official reason. This level of information would only have been divulged when they were actually en route to their destination.

One well-remembered and consistent detail that recurs in their recollections was that, on 31 July 1945, 1835 Sqn finished training and dispersed for one week's embarkation leave. This was to rest the squadron and allow a short period of home leave before the unit departed for the Far East for front-line combat duties. The aircraft were loaded aboard HMS *Patroller* at Sydenham Docks in Northern Ireland, and that was the last contact the squadron members had with them. A week later on 7 August 1945, when they returned from their leave, the atomic bomb had been dropped on Hiroshima and, with the war effectively over, 1835 Sqn was disbanded. The aircraft were unloaded from *Patroller* and the pilots and crew were dispersed to other squadrons and duties.

This seemingly insignificant detail plays a very major part in determining when the gas patch was applied to KD431 and, presumably, to other aircraft on the squadron. All of the above-mentioned pilots have visited the FAAM (individually and as a group), and all have sat in the KD431's cockpit and looked out over the port wing to view the very distinctive yellow-and-red circle that is the gas-reactive paint patch. Their conclusion is that the gas patches definitely did not exist on their aircraft up to the point at which they dispersed for leave, on 31 July 1945.

During normal flying the pilot would pay more attention to the port-side view from the cockpit than to the starboard-side view. All approaches for landing were made in a left-hand circuit, requiring an almost constant view over the front of the port wing. Flight deck control officers (batsmen) were stationed on the port side of the flight deck. In flight, with the right hand on the aircraft control column and the left hand on the throttle, it required an easier manoeuvre of the body to look out of the port side than the starboard. This would have been a very familiar view for these pilots.

It therefore seems logical to infer that the instruction to apply the gas-reactive paint was issued while the aircraft were embarked in *Patroller*. Having just undergone an intensive period of use for flying training, they would certainly have required varying amounts of servicing and adjustment, and it would be quite normal for any other modifications to be made by the squadron air fitters at this time. However, despite numerous appeals for further details, or for former air fitters to come forward with their recollections, no such information has been forthcoming.

The perceived threat of gas/chemical warfare being used by the Japanese in the closing stages of the Second World War is fairly well documented, though no documentary evidence appears to exist as to exactly what threat 1835 Sqn was likely to encounter, and where.

Certainly the circular gas-reactive patch applied to KD431's wing has prompted a great deal of interest among aircraft enthusiasts and historians. It is currently believed to be the only remaining example of its type.

RESEARCH LINKS WITH CONTINUING WORK

At this stage in the project, research and physical work on the object were proceeding concurrently. A good basic diary of the aircraft's movements had been compiled, but useful photographs of the aircraft before its arrival at Yeovilton were still proving difficult to find. It was also essential to communicate with any remaining people who were connected with KD431 either during its squadron service or while it was at Cranfield College, to help fill some of the gaps from first-hand recollections.

During the early stages of work I had issued an appeal for photographs that might show the aircraft at any time before its arrival at Yeovilton. This was carefully controlled to ensure that we were not swamped with countless images that would be of little or no use and would take valuable time to sort and return to their owners. The appeal was performed in

This study of KD431 at Cranfield College in 1958 at last provided a good-quality colour reference for comparison with the team's researches and discoveries. Involvement in this project brought appreciation of the extent to which modern colour photography is taken for granted. The yellow wide-load markers on the wings are clearly visible. (J. Halley, MBE)

stages, targeting all of the most likely sources (photo archives, societies, journals) in rotation, to allow breathing space.

This aircraft was the only Royal Navy Corsair known to exist after the Second World War. Cranfield College had staged many open days over the years, and the Corsair was a particular favourite with aircraft enthusiasts and photographers. I braced myself for an avalanche of mail, but received barely a handful of responses. Photography is now a cheap and common means of recording, and I initially failed to appreciate just how sparing, careful and thoughtful photographers were during the 1940s, 1950s and 1960s with their limited supplies of costly film and individually purchased flash bulbs. Nonetheless, I was able to gather a small collection of black-and-white images with which to work.

Most of these images were grainy and of poor quality by today's standards. However, they were vital to producing a visual time-line that would help to confirm what, if anything, had changed on the aircraft at a few known points in time (provided the photographs could be dated).

I had hoped for a colour image of the aircraft during its time in service, but thought that I would be unlikely to find one. However, some projects seem to be blessed with luck and good fortune. In February 2001 I received an envelope from James Halley, MBE, containing a very precious colour slide from his personal collection. It was a sharp, clear, three-quarter-front view of Corsair KD431, parked inside a hangar at Cranfield during the 1950s. What a find! This was a turning point in the project and the associated research.

The picture was taken in 1958, twelve years after the aircraft had arrived at the college. However, black-and-white photographs dating from the early 1950s, only a few years after it had arrived there, showed many of the same details and witness marks as the colour image. Furthermore, the few images of the aircraft dating later than the 1958 colour image also showed the same details. In addition, several former lecturers from the college all had similar recollections of the aircraft and its time there. They all remembered: 'the aircraft had spent years in the hangars being used as a wing-fold demonstrator. No one would have repainted her; there was no need. There was no facility, anyway.'

If the aircraft had survived at Cranfield largely unchanged from its in-service condition with the FAA, we now had a colour reference to this period. This image became the most important yardstick in all of our examinations to date, and for further work. So much of what we had theorised or best-guessed could now be confirmed or re-evaluated against a completely accurate reference.

Many thoughts as to which era in time we intended to capture with this exercise now seemed clearer and more defined. Focusing just on factory detail would have seen many other interesting and unique details lost during paint removal. On the other hand, the squadron Service markings are from a different era, so where does one draw the line? With such a brief time-span from factory departure to leaving FAA service (eighteen months), we all agreed that a spread of development could be captured. It would not have been as straightforward if the aircraft's Service life had spanned many years, and might have achieved a very confused result. Here, however, was a chance to uncover and 'freeze in time' a true catalogue of details and events relating to one aircraft, covering a time-span that could be tightly defined, and make sense of the few period alterations.

OUT OF THE BLUE

The project had now been well under way for about a year, and many fascinating details had been uncovered and interesting theories examined. We were always hoping for lucky breaks, and for some unexplained reason we often had them. However, it could be argued that our thorough, meticulous approach to each area was bringing in the results, rather than reliance on luck.

One afternoon, completely out of the blue, I was contacted by Eric Beechinor, a retired FAA officer. He was enquiring, on behalf of a friend living in America, as to whether the FAAM would be interested in a painting of a Corsair that his friend wished to donate to a worthy estab-

Sadly, John Foulkes's flying log book was lost many years ago. However, his FAA flying companion, Eric Beechinor, still had his log book and could confirm the deck-landing incident on HMS *Premier*. Eric flew KD431 on the morning of 27 September 1945. John then took his turn at deck landing, suffering the mishap in the afternoon of the same day. It was the subject of much friendly leg-pulling between these two friends for many years. *(Crown Copyright/MoD)*

YEAR 1945		AIRCRAFT		PILOT, OR 1ST PILOT	2ND PILOT, PUPIL OR PASSENGER	DUTY (INCLUDING RESULTS AND REMARKS)
MONTH	DATE	Type	No.			
—	—		—	—	—	— TOTALS BROUGHT FORWARD
			768	D.L.T.	SQUADRON	(BALLYHALBERT)
SEPT.	20	CORSAIR	KD280	SELF	SOLO	FERRY – NAVY BELFAST, NORTHERN IRELAND to R.N.A.S. BALLYHALBERT, N.I.
SEPT	22	CORSAIR	JT642	SELF	SOLO	LOCAL FAMILIARIZATION
SEPT	23	CORSAIR	JT686	SELF	SOLO	ADDLES AT KIRKISTON 8 APP. 8 CUTS.
SEPT	27	CORSAIR	JT218	SELF	SOLO	ADDLES AT KIRKISTON 9 APP. 8 CUTS.
SEPT	27	CORSAIR	DK431	SELF	SOLO	TO HMS "PREMIER" + RETURN 8 DECK LANDINGS
SEPT	28	BARRACUDA	—	P.O. —	SELF	R.N.A.S. BALLYHALBERT – PASSENGER TO ABBOTSINCH SCOTLAND
					GRAND TOTAL [Cols. (1) to (10)] 378 Hrs. 21 Mins.	TOTALS CARRIED FORWARD

lishment. As the description of the painting unfolded it became obvious that Mr Beechinor was also a former Corsair pilot. To our amazement it transpired that he had actually flown KD431. Log book entries for his time on 768 Sqn clearly showed the aircraft's serial number.

But what of his friend, and the painting? As the conversation progressed I was keen to understand how he had met his American friend, and how the Corsair link was formed. 'Was he a former US Marine Corps or Navy pilot?' I enquired.

'Oh, no,' came the answer. 'He is also ex-Fleet Air Arm. He and I were on the squadron together, and he emigrated to America some years ago.' His name, unbelievably, was John Foulkes, whose unfortunate deck-landing accident with KD431, resulting in the damaged propeller and wingtip, appeared on the accident record card for September 1945. I had spent over a year trying to establish if John Foulkes was still traceable, and had all but given up hope, as every trail led nowhere. Completely unaware of the project and barely familiar with the museum itself, John was about to discover (through chance, and his kind offer) that his aircraft, complete with the damage from that day in 1945, existed in an aviation museum.

Delight, disbelief and great amusement at having finally made contact in this way and put more pieces of the jigsaw into place, best sums up the telephone conversations that ensued between John Foulkes and myself. Sadly, deteriorating health and distance prevented John from being properly reunited with the aeroplane he had flown so many years ago. But I am told that photographs and a copy of his A25 accident report form brought a wry smile to the old Corsair man in his twilight months.

The information gleaned from conversations with John Foulkes was of vital importance to the project. John could recall clearly the whole sequence of events that led up to the deck-landing mishap:

It was my first deck landing. My approach was a little fast, I bounced a little and caught the last wire. I knew that I would take the barrier, you nearly always did if you were on the eighth wire. Luckily I had managed to lose a little speed and got on the brakes a little – so the damage was light. I spun a little and caught the starboard wingtip on the barrier stanchion. It was all repairable, they struck the aircraft down into the hangar and made repairs overnight. It wasn't badly damaged, I flew her off the next day.

All of John's recalled information matched the accident record card, and also confirmed the source of the damage to the starboard wingtip. His description of the repaired areas on both the wingtip and the propeller matched perfectly. More importantly, his information confirmed that the aircraft was still carrying the same mechanical components and light repairs today, unchanged from that date in 1945. We now had a lot of proof to back up our theories and speculation regarding how original we believed the forward portion of the aircraft to be.

First-hand recollection by John Foulkes proved this to be the repair carried out after the HMS *Premier* landing accident. This repair, and repairs to the damaged propeller, are now known to have been effected in the ship's hangar during the night of 27/8 September 1945. On the following day John Foulkes flew KD431 from the ship and continued his flying training with no further mishaps. *(FAAM)*

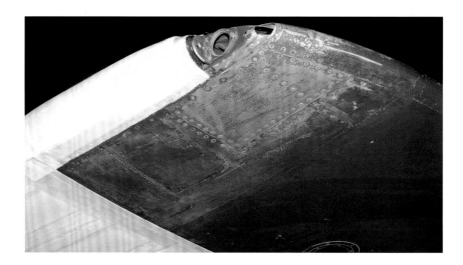

THE HANGAR PARTY

Attempts to contact ex-factory employees, squadron personnel, Cranfield College staff and relevant archivists was having limited results, both with regard to making the contacts and to the information gained thereby. We wondered whether, at this stage rather than on completion of the task, a reunion of all of those connected with KD431 might yield a result. The decision was made to stage a hangar party and invite any 1835 and 768 Sqn members who could be contacted, members of the ship's company of HMS *Premier* during 1945, former lecturers and students of Cranfield College, and any other persons whom we thought may have had close connections with KD431 between 1944 and 1963.

As a reunion the party was a huge success, reuniting old friends and comrades, some of whom had not met in nearly sixty years, and creating new friendships linked by Corsairs in general and our Corsair in particular. Former 1835 Sqn Senior Pilot J.D. Buchanan was so taken with the idea that he journeyed from his home in Canada just to be at the event. 'If the boys are re-forming for the day, then I had jolly well better be there,' was his emphatic response to my invitation. Advancing years and the vast distance from New Zealand only just prevented another 1835 Sqn pilot, John Morton, from attending. However, his personal telegram arrived at midday, to wish that he could have been there, '. . . and to convey my fond regards to all my former squadron friends'. Similarly, John Foulkes arranged for a floral tribute and message to his old comrades to arrive that day. If nothing else, the hangar party ensured that many people, across the globe, were now back in touch with each other and communicating again after nearly sixty years.

Many fascinating personal recollections came to the fore but, sadly, very little of the information regarding the details and movements of KD431 that was badly needed for the continuing research. These recollections, personal stories and remarkable coincidences are related in the chapter entitled 'Corsair Pilots Speak'.

UNDERCARRIAGE

With the wings completed, the undercarriage, undercarriage bays and wheels were the next to be closely examined.

The undercarriage bays were coated with a heavy layer of oil-impregnated grime. This appeared to be the result of dust gathering and adhering to the oil residues in the bays over many years. A thorough cleaning of this area was required if we were to establish how original the paint finish and fittings within the bays were. At this point one of the team raised a fair question. Should we remove the grime? Was it not a part of the aircraft's history, or was that going too far? We decided, as a team, that we were interested in preserving and examining the original finish, not the build-up of debris over the years. This did, however, show that the team was thinking, debating and reasoning on a different level than at the beginning of the project.

A thorough clean-out of the bays, using a citrus-based degreasing fluid, revealed extremely good paint finishes that had been concealed and protected beneath the grime for many years. On the rear of the under-carriage legs themselves, original Chrysler Corporation manufacturer's transfers still existed. These fragile white transfers state

The undercarriage bays were largely untouched in the 1963 repaint. Areas that were sprayed were protected beneath a layer of oil and grease residue, formed when the aircraft was in service. A thorough degrease and clean was all that was needed in these areas to reveal the near-perfect original factory finish. *(FAAM)*

Many rare and delicate transfers have been uncovered, demonstrating the variety of American manufacturers involved in Second World War aircraft production. *(FAAM)*

that the undercarriage units were made under licence from the Cleveland Pneumatic Tool Company, Cleveland, Ohio, USA; further evidence of licence-built products being contracted out to large manufacturing companies in the wartime production drive. Similarly, many of the smaller components in the undercarriage bay (as in the wing-fold area) revealed traces of the mid-blue used on US-paint-scheme Corsairs beneath the dark blue colour scheme of our aircraft.

Undercarriage bays are notoriously difficult to work within, clean or repaint when an aircraft is in its complete state. It was clear that these areas had not been oversprayed in 1963, and that what we were looking at, in both bays, was completely original factory paint.

Even this small area yielded a mass of information relating to the way the aircraft was manufactured and treated at various stages of construction and finishing: which areas were spray-painted, and which were missed or sprayed over as a result of inadequate masking during the factory finishing process. Many books allude to the speed at which aircraft were passed along wartime production lines. Here was the 'living book', a three-dimensional example of what had happened to an airframe during such high-speed production.

LEG PLATES

Attached to the front of each undercarriage leg is what is effectively a portion of undercarriage door. When the leg is retracted into its stowed position within the wing, this flat aluminium plate becomes part of the lower wing skin, shielding the retracted leg. Two small power-operated doors close over the remaining aperture to conceal the leg completely. When the undercarriage leg is extended this plate acts as a shield, preventing a certain amount of water, mud, stones and debris from being thrown up into the undercarriage bays during take-off and landing. With the undercarriage extended the plate provides an ideal surface upon which to paint a squadron recognition code.

Study of the reference photographs collected thus far indicated that the markings on, and indeed the background colour of, the leg plates differed from the finish we were now seeing. The 1963 repaint had again covered original squadron markings. The lettering applied to this recent paint finish on both of the plates, stencilled on in red paint, read:

**WARNING
RELEASE AIR
BEFORE DISMANTLING
UNIT AND SERVICE
ONLY AS DETAILED
IN CORPS AIR NAMO A8**

The 1835 Sqn code letter 'S' of 1945 emerges from beneath the 1963 paintwork. The 'S' had been painted first in white and then in pale blue. At this stage the significance of the colour change had yet to be fully understood. *(FAAM)*

The finished undercarriage leg plate with the fully revealed handpainted code letter 'S' from the aircraft's time in 1835 Sqn, applied more than sixty years earlier. *(FAAM)*

This was obviously an instruction warning of the immediate dangers associated with the high pneumatic pressure within the undercarriage leg.

Corps Air NAMO A8 was presumably an American reference or document familiar to squadron maintainers at the time. To date, no such reference has been found in any research material used on this project.

Close study of the plate soon revealed that this stencilled message was covering a similar hand-painted version. Also, on the port plate only, the outline of a larger letter 'S' or number '5' was faintly visible beneath a previous coat of paint. Aircraft attached to 1835 Sqn were given single-letter call-sign codes, and archive documentation confirmed that KD431 was indeed coded 'S'.

Careful paint removal soon revealed a dull, matt grey/brown colour beneath the most recent blue top coat. This matched the colour of the plate as shown in the 1958 colour image taken at Cranfield, and was also the layer upon which the handpainted repeat instruction was applied (this also matched the Cranfield image). Beneath this grey/brown coat was dark blue paint, and it was to this coat that the letter S had been applied.

Two other very interesting details emerged from this paint examination. Firstly, the letter S had initially been painted in white, the standard colour for Royal Navy aircraft markings on dark-coloured aircraft, and then repainted light blue, following the exact outline of the letter S. Secondly, a small factory-applied white ink-block stencil had been applied to the bottom left-hand corner of the plate. Referring to the aircraft tyre pressures for land-based or shipborne activities, it reads:

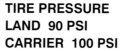

TIRE PRESSURE
LAND 90 PSI
CARRIER 100 PSI

On its own, this small, seemingly insignificant detail seems unimportant and could so easily have been rubbed away during cleaning. However, when added to the many factory-applied instructions that we were finding, it helped to build a complete and important record. This is important because, of all the complete Corsairs known to exist worldwide (currently numbering about fifty), KD431 is the only one known to retain all of its factory markings down to this level of originality and detail.

With no reference diagrams to show where factory or squadron markings might be, constant vigilance was required in order to find and save rare and original markings such as these. The stencil on the leg plate refers to aircraft tyre pressures for land or aircraft-carrier use. It reads: 'TIRE PRESSURE – LAND 90 PSI. CARRIER 100 PSI'. *(FAAM)*

Returning to the letter handpainted on the plate, this had its own fascinating and important story to tell. As mentioned, it was no surprise to find the white letter S. However, the pale blue overpainting proved much more interesting. This blue-painted S was clearly intended to be an accurate overpaint of the same letter. It was also beneath the grey/brown-painted layer, which it obviously pre-dates. Drawing a coloured diagram of the stages helped to plot and deduce the changes, date points and significance of these markings.

Research had shown that the plates were in the dull brown finish by the time the aircraft arrived at Cranfield, and were repainted dark blue on arrival at Yeovilton. Also the white S made sense from the Corsair's early

Top left to bottom right: The sequence of colour and marking modifications to the undercarriage leg plates. Drawing these out in sequence not only provided an understanding of the colour changes on the leg plates, but also provided prompts and indicators to what else might be concealed on the aircraft, in similar date/sequence order.

1. Factory primer finish.
2. Factory glossy sea blue finish with tyre pressure stencil applied.
3. First squadron code (single letter 'S') hand applied in white paint; 1835 Sqn.
4. Letter 'S' overpainted with pale blue paint for South East Asia Command; 1835 Sqn.
5. Whole plate overpainted by hand in slate grey colour; 768 Sqn.
6. Handpainted warning notice applied on to slate grey finish; 768 Sqn. *(FAAM)*

Service days with 1835 Sqn. At this stage the pale blue 'S' was not fully understood.

Paint removal on the fuselage side was also revealing similar layers, stages and colours in the region of the aircraft code lettering. Here, too, the side-letter 'S' had first been painted white and then overpainted in pale blue. This had again been painted over in dull grey/brown, but this time the letter 'M' had been applied on top of the grey/brown finish. The 'M' was part of a sequence on the fuselage side that read 'E2-M'. This was the aircraft's code when it was attached to 768 Sqn. This also made sense of the sequence change of markings, and put the pale blue 'S' (on the fuselage and leg plate) before the aircraft's time with 768 Sqn. But again, why pale blue?

The explanation was that 1835 Sqn was preparing to head for the Far East in the summer of 1945. A Confidential Admiralty Fleet Order (CAFO1099 A/A W.D 670/45 of June 1945) contains the official instructions for Royal Navy aircraft distinguishing symbols and colour changes at this time. The colour changes for side code markings in the CAFO are Sky, or Medium Sea Grey. Sky, as it is known in connection with aircraft colours, is an odd shade of light green/blue usually applied to the underside of aircraft with temperate camouflage upper surfaces. It was chosen not because it is the colour of the sky, but because, owing to the colour perception of the naked eye, it merges effectively with sky and cloud colouring at a distance.

Local interpretation and/or availability of specified colours may well have had a bearing on exactly which colour ended up on the aircraft, particularly under war conditions. Sky (aircraft colour) paint also may not have been available to a squadron equipped with aircraft that were

The fuselage-side code letter 'S' repeated the sequence of colours and alterations discovered on the undercarriage leg plates. *(FAAM)*

glossy dark blue all over. However, dark blue paint (used for the aircrafts' main finish and roundels) and white paint (aircraft codes and roundels) would have been, offering an easy mix for pale blue.

The importance of these letters and their colouring is two-fold. Firstly, they demonstrate the type of improvisation that proves that the official instruction and the actual application may differ. Secondly, we had uncovered what was almost certainly an original colour-code change, as specified for aircraft intended for South East Asia Command. Here again we were looking at (and responsible for saving) what is thought to be the only remaining authentic example of such a marking on a Second World War Royal Navy aircraft.

WHEELS AND TYRES

The wheels and tyres on KD431 proved to be a fascinating study in their own right. Comparing the details shown in our time-line of photographs with the aircraft itself soon revealed several obvious differences. Firstly, the tyres, as currently fitted were from a McDonnell Douglas F-4 Phantom jet fighter, and clearly not the tyres shown in the earlier photographs. Photographs taken between 1954 and the mid-1970s show KD431 with tyres having two distinctly different tread patterns. One is a diamond tread pattern and the other a form of raised oval pattern. These tyres were of the type used when the aircraft was in service, and date from at least the earliest reference of its being at Cranfield. The change to Phantom tyres coincided neatly with the fact that these modern FAA jet fighters were based at Yeovilton during the 1970s, and spare tyres would have been plentiful. For many years a variety of American aircraft have standardised on a wheel size of 32in × 8in, which enabled this update. The early reference photographs also clearly show that the wheels themselves were each a different colour, the port wheel being dark, probably blue, while the starboard wheel was finished in silver or natural aluminium.

What had happened to the original tyres? Had they been discarded or refitted to another aircraft? Did they still exist? The result of the next stage of investigation could be regarded as proof of the adage 'Never throw anything away. It might come in useful one day.'

This certainly applied to KD431's original tyres. Among the spare tyres held in store at the FAAM were several diamond-tread examples of the correct size and vintage. Also, fitted to the port wheel of the museum's Grumman Hellcat was an oval-tread-patterned tyre. Until we embarked on this particular project it had never occurred to me that any of these tyres might previously have been fitted to KD431. An examination to prove this required the wheels and tyres to be examined in the closest detail on both their inner and outer surfaces. Comparisons could then be made with the photographs, for witness marks such as tread wear, cuts or imperfections in the treads, and also for painted-on details such as creep marks. (These are handpainted reference points that match exactly across the junction of tyre and wheel rim. Any rotation or 'creep' of the tyre's fit and position on the wheel will immediately be noticed owing to misalignment of these marks.) Close study of all of the above yielded enough positive results to enable us to conclude, beyond doubt, that the oval-tread-pattern Hellcat tyre and one of the diamond-pattern tyres in storage were previously fitted to the Corsair wheels.

Cast into the inner surface of the wheel, as part of the manufacturing process, are a series of small notches. Positioned around the entire circumference of the inner wheel rim, they grip the bead of the inflated tyre to help prevent the tyre rotating upon its wheel (creeping) when the wheel and tyre are fitted and in use. These small grip bars (which, when studied closely under a magnifying glass, often have individual imperfections) and other imperfections in the wheel casting itself provided further witness marks that had mirrored themselves on to the tyre rubber that had been in contact with these areas. This not only provided further proof that each wheel and tyre had previously been together, but enabled us to refit the

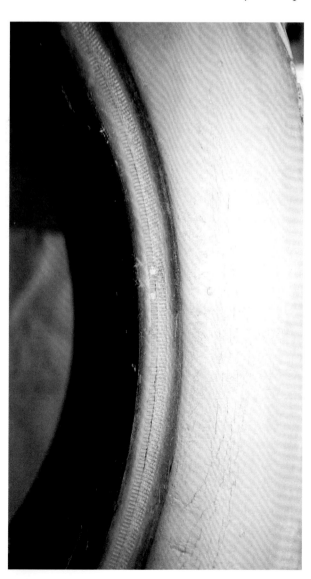

Two distinct indentations in the bead edge of the tyre. These witness marks were caused by the inflated tyre being forced under pressure against corresponding imperfections in the wheel casting for years. Would KD431's wheels have any corresponding marks? *(FAAM)*

tyres to their correct, respective wheels and in exactly the original position on that wheel. This might seem a little excessive by some standards, but if there is an opportunity to use evidence and proof to that degree of accuracy, why not use it?

The tyres were showing signs of decay and weakness, so the assumption that they had been removed for fear of failing under pressure was probably correct. What was important was that the tyres luckily had not been thrown away when they were replaced in the 1970s. With the advances in modern technology we were able to repressurise these original tyres with a liquid rubber filling and refit them safely.

As mentioned previously, early photographs showed the wheels to be finished in two different colours, the starboard wheel being silver-painted or natural aluminium and the port wheel dark (probably blue). This mismatch of wheels and tyres clearly would not have happened during the aircraft's manufacture, and Cranfield College would have had limited access to replacement wheels and tyres for American aircraft. The strong likelihood was that the change occurred during its FAA service. A study of photographs showed that Corsairs on many squadrons operated with tyres of different tread patterns on the same aircraft. This being so, was it possible to prove which, if either, was the original wheel for KD431?

Photographs taken at the Goodyear plant, showing Corsairs from similar production batches, clearly show dark-finished wheels, and we knew that these were finished in blue, to match the aircraft. Moreover, all of these aircraft have tyres with the diamond-style tread pattern. This matched what we had on the port side of KD431. Unfortunately, the Goodyear factory archive records are not sufficiently extensive to confirm which wheel casting numbers matched which aircraft numbers from the 1940s, and a lack of in-service photographs prevents positive visual identification.

The wheel had been repainted blue, but this paint was now peeling away easily. Careful work with a soft brass brush removed this later finish, exposing the original factory blue beneath and also revealing tyre-pressure references and creep line positions handpainted on the wheel. These handpainted details matched those visible on the earliest available reference photographs of the aircraft (Cranfield 1954), and almost certainly date from its time in FAA service.

Further investigation of the area between the wheel spokes revealed a red/brown waxy residue. These globules of semi-hard wax appeared to be the remains of a preservative coating, as used to protect vulnerable areas of an aircraft during long-term storage or, more appropriately, during transportation, perhaps as exposed ship's deck cargo. This tallied exactly with the residue

Another witness mark. Apparently, poor use of a tyre lever during a previous tyre removal has left a scar in the edge of the tyre bead. This might have happened in the 1970s, when these original tyres were replaced by more modern jet-aircraft tyres. *(FAAM)*

Conclusive proof. The witness marks match exactly with corresponding marks on the wheel rim itself. Similar exercises were carried out with both tyres and both wheels to prove an original match. *(FAAM)*

marks found on the wing-fold areas (and other sensitive areas), remaining from its November 1944 transatlantic crossing. The cast magnesium-aluminium alloy from which the wheels are manufactured would have been quickly damaged if exposed to salt-water spray, and would have been treated with just such a heavy-duty protective wax.

The starboard wheel, fitted to the aircraft in 1999/2000, had also been repainted blue, and careful cleaning revealed that it was indeed silver beneath. However, its spoke pattern did not match that of the starboard wheel in the 1954 photograph. The wheel on the aircraft has pairs of lugs, cast alternately into the spokes (as has the port wheel), but the photograph shows a similar-style wheel, finished in silver, but without the lugs. This was obviously not the same wheel as that fitted to the aircraft by 1954. Further detailed study of photographs finally revealed that the entire wheel and tyre assembly was cross-fitted to the museum's Grumman Hellcat during the 1970s. Unfortunately, at this stage the wheel underwent a complete paint strip and refinish, and so is no longer in the original condition from 1954 or earlier. It is, however, the same wheel and tyre, dating from the earliest reference photograph, and is now permanently refitted to KD431. Our conclusions regarding this small area are:

Comparison of the tyre and wheel details in the Cranfield photograph (inset) with the recently exposed paint finish on the aircraft's wheels helped to prove that the tyres did indeed match the wheels from the date of the earliest available photographs of KD431. These photographic references and witness marks enabled the tyres to be re-fitted to the correct wheels in exactly the correct positions. *(FAAM; J. Halley, MBE)*

1. Both wheels and tyres from earliest reference are now refitted to the aircraft in their exact positions.
2. The starboard wheel and tyre were replaced at least as long ago as 1954, and probably during FAA service.
3. The port wheel, and possibly the tyre, appear to be the original factory-fitted items, still fitted to the same side of the aircraft.

COCKPIT

Access to the cockpit is normally via the starboard side of the aircraft. Built into the wing stub and fuselage are spring-loaded steps and hand grips to enable the pilot to clamber up to this lofty position, 8ft above the ground. Later models had an extra step added to the inboard starboard flap. Many former Corsair pilots, now advanced in years, have wondered at just how athletic they must have been to achieve this climb while wearing flying clothing and a parachute.

The footstep, set into the fuselage, is marked with a vertical white stripe, spray-painted in white, leading from the top of the step aperture to the edge of the cockpit itself. This marking, which served as a guide and sight line to lead a person's foot towards the step aperture when exiting

The Corsair cockpit is generous with space, but beware, without cockpit floor plates (standard on FAA Corsairs) any dropped items would go a very long way down. *(FAAM)*

the cockpit, has been applied twice on the side of KD431. The most recent version, dating from 1963, was applied so as to be vertical when the tail of the aircraft is on the ground, and is therefore at an angle to the fuselage wall itself. The original orientation, as can be seen beneath this second application, is at a true 90 degrees to the fuselage wall.

Immediately below the starboard edge or rim of the cockpit itself, stamped into the skin of the fuselage in ¼in-high letters, is the number 1871. This number is repeated, in a similar fashion, on the immediate next panel forward, and also in the same position on the port side upper fuselage panel. The numerals appear to have been hand stamped rather than machine stamped on to the fuselage skin. As this number matches both the government contract number for Corsairs being built at this time and the aircraft's individual build number, it is unclear whether it relates to one reference (stamped twice), or whether one number represents the contract number, and the other the build number.

Corsair Bu No. 88391, a Goodyear FG-1D built to a US contract during 1944 and now privately owned and based at Duxford Airfield in Cambridgeshire, England, shows no evidence of any numbers having been stamped in this area. The same applies to Corsair FG-1A, Bu No. 13459, housed in the US Marine Corps Museum at Quantico, Virginia, in the USA, no numbers being stamped into its aluminium skin in this area. If this was an application that ceased to be a factory procedure on D-type Corsairs, one would expect it to appear on the earlier A-type at Quantico.

Above: View of the right-hand side of KD431's cockpit wall. Note the canvas signal pistol holster still fitted to the side-wall framework.

Opposite, top: KD431's cockpit is still in remarkable condition. Even the compass correction card (top right) appears to date from its last flights more than sixty years ago.

Below: Many of the cockpit's original items of electrical and radio equipment are still fitted and intact. (FAAM)

Research to date has failed to determine whether this form of numbering is specific to British-contract Corsairs, or whether date point, aircraft type or other reasons might provide an explanation.

The sliding cockpit hood, or canopy, is designed to enable release and opening from the starboard side. Three types of canopy were used on different marks of Corsair. The 'bird-cage' type fitted to early Corsairs is recognisable by the multiple glazing bars in the canopy sides, to retain the Perspex portions.

The first canopy was succeeded by the 'semi-blown' type, accompanied by a change in cockpit seating height. This design dispensed with the numerous glazing bars, replacing them with two larger, high-mounted ribs that held three separate Perspex portions in place. These were noticeably more curved, allowing the pilot a much clearer and less interrupted view. Later marks had the 'fully-blown' canopy with no glazing strips and a more pronounced curvature to the Perspex, giving the pilot an even better view.

Corsair KD431 has the correct semi-blown sliding canopy for a 1944 production aircraft. However, there is contradictory evidence (and opinion, if you compare the Goodyear documents with the US Navy Bureau number details) regarding which mark of Corsair KD431 actually is. Depending on which document you choose to believe, the aircraft is either an FG-1A or an FG-1D. The semi-blown canopy would be correct for an FG-1A, but at least one reference book suggests that D-type

Another number conundrum, yet to be solved. Close examination reveals the number 1871 stamped twice into the aircraft's fuselage skin. Are they the fabrication number and contract number, or is it the fabrication number stamped twice? The only other FG-1A in existence has no numbers stamped in these positions. Neither do any FG-1Ds that have been available for research to date. *(FAAM)*

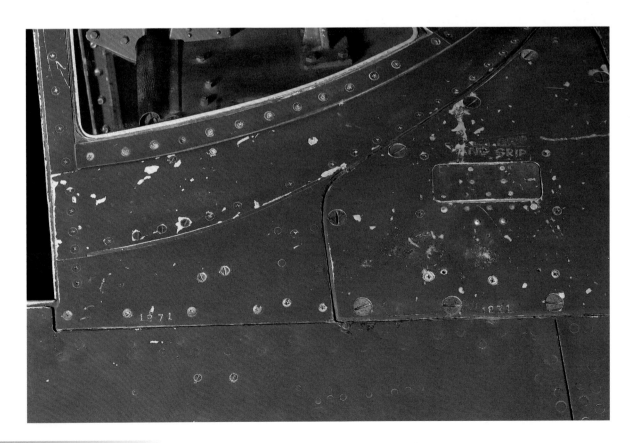

Corsairs were fitted with A-type canopies on the production line until old stock was used up. While this is an entirely reasonable theory, it should not automatically be used to determine the mark number of any particular Corsair.

Removal of the canopy for thorough examination, cleaning and paint treatment revealed more fascinating details that had been painted over and concealed since 1963.

Written in pencil on the inside of the sliding portion of canopy was the number '431', another reference to our specific aircraft. The style of this

Unearthed from beneath the neatly marked-out 1963 refinish, these canopy emergency cut lines were handpainted and gauged by eye when first applied in 1945. Note the original factory 'ENCLOSURE RELEASE' transfer and the crudely applied yellow paint on the inner canopy joint line, also added in 1945. *(FAAM)*

handwritten numbering matched the style of similar handwritten references elsewhere on the aircraft, giving the impression that this, too, had been applied in the Goodyear factory. Certainly this inner-face portion of the canopy is shielded from view at all times when the canopy is fitted, in both the open and closed positions. Until the canopy was removed as part of the investigation it was impossible to see this inscription.

On the outside of the canopy, following the frame edge, a series of rectangular painted blocks mark the line along which to cut to remove a jammed canopy in an emergency. These yellow block marks had been applied in 1963, on top of the then resprayed blue finish, having been carefully marked out with masking tape before being neatly sprayed. Close examination and removal of some of the 1963 blue finish soon revealed hand-applied yellow emergency-cut-line markings beneath. Much less uniform in shape and positioning, they still bear the brush strokes from their application. Photographs indicate that this marking was added during the aircraft's time with 768 Sqn, which also tallies with written references indicating that such markings were being applied from May 1945 onwards.

On the starboard side of the canopy forward vertical frame is the remains of a factory-applied transfer (decal) reading 'ENCLOSURE RELEASE'. This has been applied with the lettering at 90 degrees to the vertical of the frame itself. The background of the transfer was originally white. No other traces of colour are visible, and it appears that the letters of the transfer were either transparent or left open to show the dark blue canopy frame colour beneath.

On the inside of the canopy frame the same yellow paint has been used to mark the emergency-cut area of the canopy frame. This has been very crudely applied by brush, and uses a continuous rather than a broken line.

It would be impractical to list details of all the cockpit fittings, and these are best shown in clear photographs. However, some details are worthy of note or further explanation.

The original pilot's seat from KD431 had not been in the aircraft since at least 1981, and research indicates that it had not been fitted in the aircraft for many years before this date. Whether the aircraft arrived from Cranfield with its seat is not known. The seat now fitted is a Corsair seat of the correct pattern, but not the original item. Some of the seat framework has been replicated to enable the replacement seat to be installed in the cockpit.

The armour-plate shield immediately behind the seat, to which the seat is in effect fitted, shows more interesting evidence of factory fitting.

Handpainted on this large steel plate is the number 1888, applied in the same way as the handpainted number discovered previously on the supercharger intakes. However, 1888 was the build number of Corsair KD449, seventeen places behind KD431 on the production line. Research shows that KD449 was delivered to 1831 Sqn in Nowra, Australia, and did not operate in close association with 1835 Sqn or KD431. The only logical explanation is that the plate was fitted (or switched) on the factory production line, but the reason is unknown. (Corsair build-number 1888

Opposite: A close-up of the armour plated seat-back shield marked 1888. The component face-stamped 'REAR' has been fitted facing forwards. Clearly it could be installed either way round, and this provides further evidence of the production-line speed in the Goodyear factory as far as the fitting of non-critical components was concerned. (FAAM)

(KD449) is recognised as being an FG-1A, providing further evidence to suggest that KD431 was the same.)

The steel armour plate is of a symmetrical shape, as are the mounting holes for the seat brackets and fuselage mounting points. This becomes more obvious when one sees the word 'REAR' stamped into the face of the steel plate that is now the front face as fitted in the cockpit. Close study of the fasteners holding the plate into position, and the lack of abrasive marks on the surrounding paintwork, indicate strongly that the plate was fitted this way in the factory.

Behind the armour plating at the rear of the seat, and spanning the entire aperture of the fuselage tube, there should be a canvas/leathercloth curtain. This fabric screen was fitted in an attempt to reduce carbon-monoxide gases from being drawn into the cockpit during flight. Exhaust gases from the rearward-facing streamlined exhaust pipes could be sucked into the fuselage and cockpit of the aircraft, with serious consequences for the pilot.

The carbon-monoxide curtain of KD431 was cut out at some point, leaving the outside edge of the curtain fixed beneath the sandwich plate on the fuselage. Oddly, the curtain itself, now reduced in size, was found discarded in the rearmost part of the fuselage. There seems to be little reason for its removal, and evidently no attempt made to replace it. It is thought that this ill-considered removal was carried out during the aircraft's earlier days at the museum, when there might have been an attempt to investigate the rear fuselage area. It is sad that this damage occurred, but at least the remains of the original curtain survive.

Above: An original factory installation, this bullet-proof armoured seat-back shield has been taken from Corsair fabrication number 1888, serial number KD449. A canvas screen to prevent carbon monoxide ingress into the cockpit was also factory-fitted behind this plate as standard. *(FAAM)*

The carbon–monoxide problem was also tackled in two other areas of the aircraft, immediately connected to the cockpit area. All of the removable panels immediately in front of the cockpit windscreen have been refitted on a thin bed of black rubberised caulking compound. This was a direct attempt to prevent the deadly exhaust gases from entering the cockpit by this route. Research has shown that this particular preventative treatment was carried out at Aldergrove in Northern Ireland, as part of the British update and refit programme carried out before the aircraft was released to squadron service. Most of KD431's forward panels still have traces of this black sealing compound around their joints. Photographs of Corsairs in service often show these forward joints taped over in an attempt to prevent the ingress of exhaust gas.

On each side of the fuselage at mid-height, just aft of the pilot's seat, there is a forward-facing air scoop, approximately 2in tall and protruding 3in out from the fuselage. These scoops gather air and funnel it into the rear portion of the fuselage, behind the carbon-monoxide curtain. The theory is that this clean air, drawn from an uncontaminated area of the slipstream, was used to create a slightly pressurised rearward airflow in the rear fuselage, thereby preventing the internal build-up of exhaust gases in this area. This fitment appears to have been factory applied, but only to British-contract aircraft. American aircraft had smaller flush-fitting vents, where applied.

Scoops on each side of the fuselage allow airflow through the inner portion of the rear fuselage to help prevent a build-up of deadly carbon-monoxide exhaust gas in the cockpit area. *(FAAM)*

A view showing the position of the scoops in relation to the fuselage-side roundel. These protruding scoops were fitted to British-specification Corsairs only. Corsairs built to US specification had flush-fitting, streamlined vents in similar positions. *(FAAM)*

Other British modifications at this stage would have included the substitution (or fitting) of British-type radio and communication systems and other minor instrument changes to suit British requirements.

The instrument panel is original, though research shows that some of the instruments were removed either at Cranfield or during the early days at the museum. This appears to be limited to the clock, compass, altimeter and gunsight. The compass correction cards, however, are still in their clear plastic holders, mounted to the dashboard. These aged buff cards, which would be filled in by hand to indicate deviations in compass readings, appear to be completely original from KD431's last flight in 1945.

There should also be a small metal plate fixed to the instrument panel, with the aircraft Bureau number stamped on it. Unfortunately this plate does not exist, and, as previously mentioned, the Bureau number has only been deduced from numbers in listings. There should also be a Goodyear manufacturer's plate inside the cockpit, confirming such details as aircraft type, manufacturer's number, customer number, original engine number and date of manufacture. On Goodyear-built Corsairs this plate would normally be fitted to the inside of the fuselage skin, immediately behind the throttle-quadrant assembly on the port side of the cockpit. No such plate exists in KD431's cockpit, and the lack of witness marks or rivet holes indicates that no such plate was ever fitted in this position.

Towards the rear of the cockpit on the port side, but positioned much higher (just below the sliding canopy rail), there are witness marks where a plate was riveted into position and, at some later stage, crudely removed using some form of blade or lever. Score marks indicate that six levering actions were necessary to prise the plate from its mounting face, leaving the rivets in place. The measurements of the plate (shadow marks) and its fixing rivets closely match the dimensions of the plate in the cockpit of the US-specification FG-1D at Duxford. They are also similar to the measurements of the 'Modification-Changes' plates that appear on different parts of the aircraft, though it seems that these were normally affixed with screws to permit updating and changing, rather than being permanently fixed with rivets. This indicates that KD431, if not all British-contract Corsairs, had manufacturer's information plates fitted in this alternative position.

More importantly, the aircraft is now missing some of its vital original components. It can only be hoped that anyone reading this who has any knowledge of the whereabouts of this plate, or of the distinctive oval-shaped Briggs Industries plate removed from the port wing, will do their utmost to ensure that either or both are returned to the FAAM (anonymously, if necessary, and with no questions asked).

On the port side of the cockpit, riveted to the front face of the main fuselage frame, is a black-and-silver plate with the words 'CHANGES INCORPORATED'. It carries hand-stamped numbers, applied in the

Difficult enough to read and all but impossible to stamp in its installed position, this modification plate tells a great deal about factory working practices and references. *(FAAM)*

appropriate spaces provided on the plate, relating to details, specifications or changes associated with this particular fuselage. This is quite normal, and this type of plate is of a standard style for the Corsair. Interestingly, in the space marked 'MODEL', it is stamped: MODEL TYPE FG-1B AIRPLANE. There has never been an official FG-1B designation for a Corsair, though American factory workers involved in Corsair production used the term FG-1B as a factory-floor reference for British-contract aircraft. Certainly the Briggs plates fitted to the wings are stamped 'BRIT.', but after the correct type designation, for example F4U-1 – BRIT. The position of the plate is such that it can only just be accessed to read. Stamping the plate after it had been riveted in place would not have been possible. It therefore appears that the convenient factory-floor reference to 'B types' for British aircraft was carried through to the stamping of factory-fitted modification plates.

Installed to the lower left-hand side of the pilot's seat is a pair of high-pressure carbon-dioxide bottles. These are of interest as objects and as part of the aircraft's systems, but the most significant discovery was two dated tags affixed to the bottle necks.

The bottles acted as high-pressure reservoirs of inert gas to perform either of two tasks. Firstly, they provided a high-pressure charge to operate the emergency undercarriage release in the event of hydraulic system

Officially there were no 'B'-type model Corsairs. However, British Corsairs were often referred to as 'FG-1Bs' among the factory production-line workers. This fuselage modification plate proves that such factory-floor invented terms were not just casually used by contract parts suppliers and production-line staff, but actually found their way in to official references. *(FAAM)*

Fitted around the necks of the two high-pressure CO2 cylinders in the floor of the cockpit, and probably not touched since installation, these inspection and fitting tags provide valuable evidence for the aircraft's exact build date. *(FAAM)*

A manufacturer's dispatch ticket attached to the bottle neck gives the date of manufacture/factory delivery of this component to Goodyear as 21 June 1944. The metal tag attached to the bottle neck gives the Goodyear production-line inspection/ fitting-to-aircraft date of 10 July 1944. *(FAAM)*

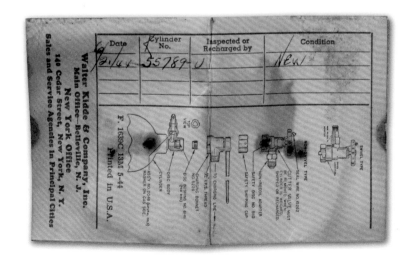

failure. Secondly, they could be used to purge any remaining fuel, air locks or fuel vapour from the fuel tanks in the outer portion of each wing. This was a common-enough installation in its day but, as most Corsairs have had the wing tanks removed, very few Corsairs (if any) remain with this entire system complete and intact.

The two tags attached around the necks of the bottles provided the most important clues to an exact factory production-line date for KD431. One tag is a brown cardboard manufacturer's tag showing that the bottle was released from the Kidde-Graviner company in New York on 21 June 1944. This ticket, still in its protective see-through celluloid wallet, is attached to the neck of the bottle with string. As well as stating the date of release from the manufacturer, it describes the bottle condition as 'NEW'.

The second tag is even more significant. It is an aluminium factory inspection tag, date-stamped 10 July 1944. This tag is typical of the type of identification used by a factory inspector to approve the installation and fitting of such equipment, and strongly indicates that the aircraft was under assembly at that time. This information, combined with the other evidence accumulated during the project, helped determine the aircraft's exact build date.

REAR FUSELAGE

The obvious areas of rear fuselage to investigate were the side areas bearing the repainted squadron codes. Evidence of previous code letters and markings could be seen below the 1963 surface when it was examined carefully in different light conditions. This, plus the desire to prove the Ceylon Corsair story, had occupied my thoughts regarding this whole project on numerous occasions.

Working rearwards, away from the cockpit, much of the fuselage work entailed straightforward but careful rubbing away of the later paint finish. With the cockpit canopy removed for separate treatment and study, the completely original paint finish on the previously shielded area of fuselage could be seen and used as a direct colour reference. One observation made during the earlier stages of fuselage work was now becoming more pronounced. This was the colour difference between the wings and the fuselage. Although we were looking at original 1944 paintwork on both areas, the colour tones were definitely different, the wings appearing to be finished in a slightly darker and greyer tone of blue. This could be due to different batches of paint being used from factory stock, or to the wings supplied by the Briggs Aviation Company being pre-finished at that factory, using completely different paint to that used by Goodyear. Production-line images of US-contract Corsairs clearly show pre-finished wings fitted to primer-coated fuselage sections on the production line. If this were the case, it would be interesting to know which company applied the British insignia roundels to the upper and lower wing surfaces. Sadly, this information is lacking. The ink-block stencilling on the wings certainly matches the stencilling on the fuselage, as per the Goodyear factory work, and even repeats the odd double-stamping irregularity on the fuselage, so these markings, at least, appear to have been applied at the Goodyear factory.

On the port side of the fuselage, on the outer surface, where the rear of the wing meets the fuselage skin, there is a small red recessed disc made of a celluloid plastic material. This disc acts as a visual (blow-out) indicator when the emergency carbon-dioxide undercarriage release has been activated.

Also on the port side of the fuselage wall are two small black-and-white engraved plates of a plastic-type material, indicating c.g. points. The centre-points of the plates are exactly 106½in apart. These plates are evident in photographs of the aircraft at Cranfield College as early as 1954, and it is known that many British aircraft of this period had c.g. reference plates fitted. What is not known is whether these plates were fitted at the Goodyear factory, on arrival in Britain (at the receiving RNAY), on either of the two squadrons with which the aircraft served, or at the college as part of the students' studies. Without a photograph showing the port side of the aircraft during its time in service, it is impossible to date the fitting of these items accurately.

Both plates are riveted to the aircraft's skin in exactly the same way, and the bare ends of the cut rivets, on the inside of the fuselage skin, have had no primer coat treatment. Research, and discussions with former Goodyear employees, yielded no reference to any such items being fitted at the factory. This is currently the only indication that this might have been a post-factory fitment, but it is by no means conclusive.

Some painted fuselage-side markings, other than the ink-block-applied instruction stencils, would have been applied in the factory. These would have been the British insignia roundel (type C1, 54in diameter, bordered in yellow) central on each side of the fuselage; the aircraft's serial number, KD431; the words 'ROYAL NAVY', positioned just below and forward of the tailplane; and the footstep guide stripe on the starboard cockpit side only.

The squadron codes would have been applied by each individual squadron as appropriate. Nowadays, aircraft are frequently completely stripped of paint between squadrons, so a build-up of code layers does not always occur. In this case, however, there was obviously a build-up, offering the chance to remove the layers and discover how squadron markings were really applied and altered on an active Second World War squadron. Again it was all too easy to fall into the trap of accepting that they were just painted on. In simple terms that was true, but closer study provided a wealth of quality information about Second World War colours and markings that survive in truly original condition on very few aircraft of this vintage, if any.

Working down through the paint layers, we discovered that three code-letter sequences had been applied to the aircraft, and that they all still existed. The work of uncovering and investigation obviously progressed from the top layer down, but for ease of explanation it is best to begin with the bottom layer (first application) and finish with the most recent.

The aircraft had first been coded with a single letter 'S' while with 1835 Sqn from January 1945 to September 1945. It was then recoded 'E2-M' when attached to 768 Sqn at East Haven, Scotland, from October 1945 until its military service ended in December 1945. When it arrived at Yeovilton in 1963 it was then repainted with new 'E2-M' codes.

To date, only one photograph is known to exist showing KD431 in flight, taken during its time with 1835 Sqn. The picture was taken by the unknown pilot of another Corsair of 1835 Sqn flying in close formation. The serial number KD431 is not visible, but the code letter 'S' can be seen. This might seem a weak and dubious assumption to use as proof, but modern technology and careful measuring has provided evidence that is difficult to refute.

Good-quality digital images were made of the original photograph and enlarged to provide a more useful size from which to scale measurements. The exact shape of the letter 'S' was then drawn to scale on a large piece of tracing paper to match the full-size letter 'S' on the side of KD431. When the tracing was overlaid on the fuselage letter, the match in shape, size and individual features of this hand-applied character was very accurate. The top of the 'S' is heavier in line than the lower portion, the ends of the 'S' finish in slightly different ways, and the line widths vary slightly. This was encouraging, but still not conclusive enough to serve as indisputable proof.

We returned to the images and repeated the exercise, this time taking horizontal and vertical reference measurements from different points on

Careful removal of the layers of paint that had built up on the various squadron codes was vital to understanding and matching the research with physical evidence. *(FAAM)*

Work in progress on the starboard fuselage side of KD431. Most of the blue paint has been cleaned back to the original factory-applied finish, only a small area around the serial number KD431 being uncompleted. The roundel and fuselage-side code letters 'E2-M' are still in the 1963 polyurethane finish, though work is just beginning on the 'M' to reveal what is beneath. Because of the positioning of the white-painted footstep stripe, the whole code has been applied aft of the roundel on this side of the fuselage. *(FAAM)*

the 'S' to reference points on the fuselage, such as the centre of the
roundel, the edge of the footstep stripe, and the outer edge of the roundel
(top and side reference points). The matched scaled dimensions to any of
these reference points came to within ½in of any point, vertical or horizontal, on the corresponding points on the aircraft. Allowing a small
margin of error for image reproduction and scaling, this, combined with
the direct mapping of the letters, seemed to be proof enough.

Although this exercise did not yield any vital information on KD431, it
demonstrated that proof of identity can be established in different ways,
and confirmed that at least one picture existed of KD431 in service. If only
we knew who was driving.

The original single code letter 'S' had been applied by brush, using white
paint, directly on to the factory-blue fuselage paint, with no priming or
surface preparation. This was the same on both sides of the aircraft. These
code letters had then been overpainted with pale blue at a later stage, again
by hand, exactly following the outline of the original white letters. This

whole sequence, and the colour blue, tallied exactly with what we had discovered on the undercarriage leg plate, and there was every reason to believe that the changes to these markings occurred at or around the same time. Here again we were looking at a colour-code change from white (standard scheme) to pale blue, the new scheme for aircraft intended for operation with South East Asia Command. This was possibly the last truly authentic surviving example of such a colour change.

The next interesting discovery was that the single 'S' code letters had been painted over, to blank them out, before the new 768 Sqn code, 'E2-M' was applied. This had not been carefully done, by spraying over with dark blue paint, as one might expect, but had been brush-painted by hand using grey/brown camouflage paint. These brown-painted square areas had clearly been laid out by hand, with little attempt at accuracy. The 768 Sqn code 'E2-M' was then applied in white, with the 'E2' positioned on the blue fuselage and the letter 'M' located, on each side of the fuselage, inside the grey/brown square covering the earlier 'S'.

The code letters themselves also provide further fascinating evidence of how tasks were performed in daily life on a second-line squadron immediately postwar. The 'E2' part of the code appears to have been marked out quite accurately on both sides of the aircraft, whereas the two 'M's have been crudely applied. Not only do these letters not match the style adopted for the 'E2' part of the code, but they do not match one another, side for side.

The positioning of the whole code is also worth noting. On the port side the code is positioned with the 'E2' separated from the 'M' by the roundel, which was correct for this period of British naval aircraft markings. On the starboard side, however, the code has been applied with the whole 'E2-M' positioned aft of the roundel. This deviation from standard appears to have been an attempt to avoid incorporating the white-painted footstep stripe into the code, which would have made it read 'E2-1M' when seen from a distance.

Numerous questions arise. Did two or more people apply separate parts of the code? Did two separate crews mark different sides of the aircraft? Did one person go along a line of aircraft, painting over the single code letters with a brown square, followed by crews painting the new codes? Did the required drying time for the brown-painted squares force a hasty finish to the job at a later stage? Did an entirely different shift of fitters finish the job with less care? Did shortages of the correct colour blue paint force the use of the relatively neutral grey/brown colour to blank out the old code?

We will probably never know the answers, and the list of possibilities is almost endless. What we do know for certain is that, in late 1945, while operating on an FAA squadron, this aircraft was carrying a code marking layout and colour arrangement contrary to most textbook descriptions and not even matching on each side of the aircraft.

Truly authentic and original Second World War markings were obviously not as important in 1963 as having a spruced-up, freshly painted aircraft to exhibit in the newly opening FAAM. This is understandable, considering that this would be the first aircraft in the museum's collection. Thus it was that, at this stage, the tired, war-worn (but completely original) KD431 received its tidy-up respray and an updated version of the 'E2-M' code. This latest version (applied in white spray-painted polyurethane) saw the positioning of the entire port-side code moved rearwards, behind the roundel, to match the starboard-side code layout.

The original 1940s code letters on KD431 have now been uncovered, revealing a completely accurate example of such markings from this period. Nothing faked or replicated, but original markings from 1944/5, with the brush marks as left by the person who applied them. This valuable (possibly unique) reference shows the full 'E2-M' on the starboard side of the aircraft, with the single 'S' code letter beneath. On the port side the partial code letter 'S' is deliberately exposed through the 'E2-M' to show the colour changes and allow this other authentic marking to be studied.

These discoveries also proved that the aircraft as a whole continued to exist in original 1944/5 condition as far along as the middle fuselage portion.

The final significant discovery concerning these markings refocuses on the original question: was this aircraft flown back from Ceylon by Godfrey Woodbine-Parish? Had this aircraft been attached to 757 Sqn at Puttalam it would almost certainly have had the unit's recognised squadron code applied to each side of the fuselage. This would have been a letter 'P' followed by an individual recognition number. This code, by date sequence, could only have existed before (i.e. beneath) the single 'S' of 1835 Sqn, and, as our physical evidence now proves, no other codes have ever been applied to this aircraft. Sadly, therefore, it must be concluded that this aircraft did not make this epic flight.

On the starboard side of the fuselage is a small sheet-metal skin repair in the fuselage wall. It is not known exactly how this damage came about, but comparison of photographs proves that it occurred while the Corsair was at Cranfield College, and was repaired at Yeovilton.

During the paint removal process, 'up-hill' paint runs were discovered in several

The code E2-M applied over the original in 1963 was intended to tidy up the appearance of the aircraft. The incorrect positioning of the whole code aft of the roundel was presumably done to match the positioning on the starboard side of the fuselage. Here, work on the letter 'M' is just beginning to remove this 1963 code. (J. Coombes)

The fully exposed original code
E2-M shows the exact position,
style, size and remains of the
original 1945 marking on the
port side of the fuselage.
Note the slate-grey colour used
by 768 Sqn to paint over the
letter 'S' of the previous unit,
1835 Sqn. (FAAM)

different areas of the fuselage. Careful examination showed that these runs were in the primer coat and not in the top coat. Many of these runs were also towards the tail of the aircraft, and on various different panels. We initially thought that the whole fuselage tube section was sprayed with its primer coat while inverted or on a rotating support cradle. This theory would have explained the uphill paint runs, but did not tally with the Goodyear factory production line and paint finishing practice. Accurate details are currently not available, but it now appears that the aluminium fuselage skins were pre-sprayed with primer while hung in various orientations, including inverted, before being riveted or spot-welded to the main fuselage frame. The result is indeed an odd display of paint runs showing through in the final finish. From the viewpoint of authenticity, though, the rear portion of the aircraft carries its own factory witness marks, proving that this area of the aircraft is again completely original and unchanged from 1944.

THE CORSAIR'S TAIL

The tail section of KD431 continued to provide many puzzles that required a vast amount of research, theorising and head scratching to make any sense of what we were finding. The colour schemes that we uncovered as the removal of 1963 paint on the tail progressed were

143

fascinating, and caused us to re-examine many different areas of the aircraft in an attempt to understand fully its origin and provenance.

The fuselage tail section, or at least part of it, was manufactured by Woodall Industries of Detroit, Michigan, USA. A manufacturer's plate bearing this company's name and address is affixed to the inside wall of the tailwheel retraction bay.

Herbert James Woodall, a talented engineer in his own right, worked on various projects connected with early automobile designs between 1912 and 1916. In 1919 he set out on his own venture, supplying precision-cut cardboard and fibreboard components for the now expanding motor industry. By 1929 Woodall Industries had been formed, and the company expanded over the next ten years to develop many new techniques and products that would make a significant contribution to the fibreboard, and, ultimately, plastics industry as a whole.

With its substantial production plant at Monro, Detroit, Woodall was an obvious choice for the US government when it was seeking to place high-volume wartime contracts for the supply of components to the major manufacturing companies. Setting up production and assembly lines to produce formed aluminium parts, Woodall Industries excelled in meeting its wartime contract targets for the manufacture of aircraft components and other essential items. Such was its success that it received the prestigious Army-Navy E Award for productivity in 1944. At peak production Woodall was engaged in the manufacture of more than 7,000 different aircraft parts for various American fighters and bombers. In February 1970 the company was absorbed into the Libby-Owen-Ford Group, which continues to this day.

The aircraft's horizontal tail surfaces are interchangeable; a starboard (or port) unit can be removed from that side, turned over and fitted to the

Sections of Corsair tailplanes were manufactured by Woodall Industries, an industrial manufacturing company based in Detroit, Michigan, USA. This is further evidence of just how diverse the choice of wartime aircraft parts contractors could be. *(FAAM)*

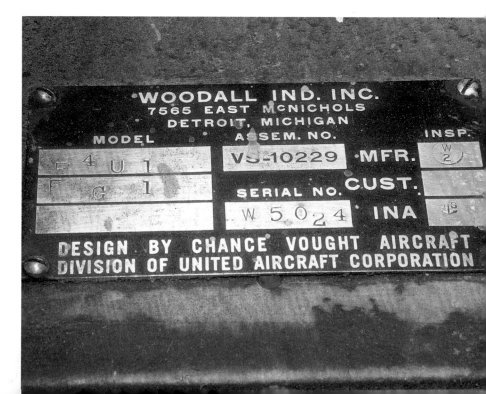

other side of the aircraft. This blissfully simple design arrangement has two major benefits. Firstly, the factory has to tool up for only one tail-plane section, not handed pairs. Secondly, replacement of a damaged part in the field is made that much easier by this universal-fit system, and fewer spares would need to be carried.

The main horizontal surfaces of the tailplane unit are aluminium skinned, while the elevators are fabric covered. Similarly, the vertical fixed fin is aluminium skinned, while the rudder is fabric covered.

The fin and rudder had not received a heavy paint coating during the 1963 repaint. Perhaps time constraints and the lack of steps of a suitable height prevented a more thorough job being done in this area. Whatever the reason, these surfaces were cleaned back to the original factory finish far easier than the fuselage and wing areas. Even the vertical red-and-blue British fin marking, overpainted with polyurethane, was easier to clean away, leaving a better result than on the wing and fuselage roundels.

On some of the vertical tail-surface panels, horizontal paint runs were found. Again these were in the primer finish, and again they provided evidence that many of the aircraft's panels were pre-sprayed in their primer coat before fitting and assembly.

The tailwheel unit and rear undercarriage assembly were in very good original condition and finish, requiring little or no paint removal to provide original surface finishes. The tailwheel and tyre, though now showing signs of deterioration (and awaiting similar treatment to the mainwheel tyres) dates at

A variety of techniques were experimented with and used to remove the 1963 paint painstakingly inch by inch from the whole aircraft. The overall approach was often more akin to archaeology and fine-art restoration than to that normally associated with aircraft engineering and restoration. *(FAAM)*

least from the aircraft's time in military service, and may well be the very item fitted in the Goodyear factory.

The fabric covering on the starboard elevator had been removed during the aircraft's time at Cranfield. As with the starboard wing, this was to allow the college students to observe the internal structure and operating linkages within the elevator section. Once uncovered, this elevator remained exposed for the duration of the aircraft's time at Cranfield, being re-covered on its arrival at Yeovilton. As with the wing, this repair was a basic repair, with no attempt to replicate the cut or layering of fabric as per the original (factory-finish) port surface.

Removal of this 1963 fabric work allowed an internal view of the elevator structure, some parts of which were ink stamped (in purple ink) with the US Navy initials and anchor motif. Having the factory-original port unit to copy when the surface was again re-covered enabled the work to be replicated exactly, almost to the stitch.

While the elevator was removed for repair and study, an interesting multiple paint scheme on the tail unit began to appear. This discovery opened up a whole series of questions and debates (worldwide) as to how this aircraft came to have this odd sequence of paint finishes.

Behind the hinged elevator portion, on the previously hidden part of the tailplane surface, three different colour schemes could be seen. The most recent was the dark glossy sea blue, as per the remainder of the aircraft. Immediately below this was olive green, and showing through beneath the green was mid-blue, as per the US Navy three-tone blue scheme.

The dark blue, matching the remainder of the aircraft, made perfect sense. The US Navy three-tone blue scheme (some undersurface areas of

With the elevator removed from the tailplane, traces of the three colour schemes applied to this unit were revealed. The parallel (horizontal) olive green overspray line indicates that the tail was sprayed in the camouflage green scheme (over the pre-finished US mid-blue scheme) with the elevators assembled and fitted to the aircraft. The big questions are whether this was done at the Brewster factory, and whether this tail and other components were then stripped from an aircraft of the terminated Brewster contract and shipped to Akron, Ohio, in June 1944 for incorporation in the newly commissioned British Corsair line at the Goodyear factory. *(FAAM)*

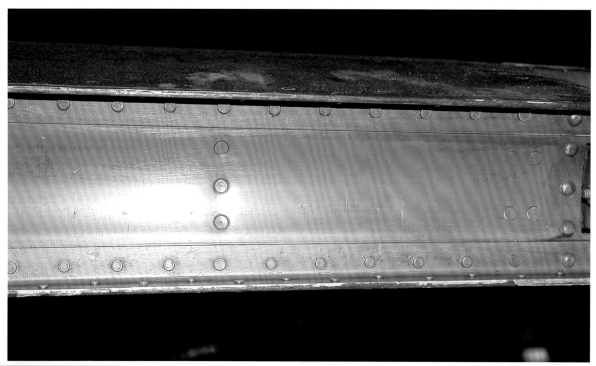

the tail were now revealing matt white, in accordance with the three-tone scheme) also made sense, if the tail had been part of a pre-sprayed factory batch, oversprayed at the final paintwork stage in the factory (as per the small wing-fold area components).

It was the addition of the olive green that prompted further questions. As more of the tailplane surfaces were carefully cleaned, a dull grey/brown colour began to emerge, with the olive green on the upper surface and duck egg colour ('sky', as it was known on British military aircraft) on the lower surface. This combination of colours was undoubtedly the British temperate camouflage scheme. It showed all the hallmarks of a factory-applied finish, but, as it had been applied to an aircraft from a factory that did not produce temperate-colour-schemed aircraft, this did not make sense.

At this stage a brief recap regarding who made what, and in what colour scheme, is required, to enable a better understanding of the subsequent thought processes.

The Vought Company made three-tone (dark blue, mid-blue and white) US-schemed aircraft, and also finished some early British-contract aircraft in the temperate camouflage scheme. However, by June 1944 the USA had standardised its colour scheme for naval aircraft to overall dark glossy sea blue, under Specification SR-2e. This also applied (from that date) to all American-built naval aircraft for supply to Britain's FAA. This is recognised in CAFO 618 (Aircraft colour and markings) of April 1945.

The Brewster Aircraft Company produced three-tone blue US-schemed aircraft, and also temperate-camouflage-schemed Corsairs for British contracts. It did not, however, remain in business long enough to produce overall dark blue Corsairs, and ceased to function as an aircraft factory at the end of June 1944.

The Goodyear company initially produced US three-tone schemed Corsairs and then standardised on overall dark blue for both US and British aircraft, under the SR-2e specification change. However, and very importantly for our findings, Goodyear did not produce any temperate (green/brown and sky) camouflage-schemed Corsairs, and started its production run of British Corsairs in the overall glossy blue finish.

Returning to our paintwork puzzle on KD431, we had to consider all of the available evidence to help explain how a green-camouflaged tail (and ammunition tanks) ended up on an all-blue aircraft.

○ Firstly, we were only dealing with an eighteen-month period from factory (July 1944) to end of service (December 1945), for at least four months of which the aircraft was at holding units or in transit to the UK. It was then ferried to at least three different units for commissioning into service and final delivery to its first squadron in January 1945. If any damage occurred in service to necessitate a tailplane change, it would have to have happened within this short period.

○ All three different colour schemes applied to KD431's tail appeared to have been professionally, factory applied.

○ The starboard tailplane had a modification changes plate affixed to its outer tip, but this had not been stamped with dates or information in the spaces. This could be taken as evidence of the tailplane not having been modified or refitted, if the plate was not carrying a date stamp or modification details.

○ It could be seen from overspray witness marks that the original US three-tone blue had been applied to the surfaces before they were fitted to an aircraft.

○ Overspray marks from the olive green paint finish showed that this coat was applied with both of the elevators fitted to the tailplanes. (It is difficult to imagine how this sequence might have occurred if they were not fitted to an aircraft.)

○ Importantly, the temperate camouflage finish appeared to match side-for-side, and gave every indication that the surfaces were sprayed as a pair, and (as confirmed by the overspray marks) would have required the units to have been fitted to an aircraft.

○ The dark blue finish on top of the temperate camouflage had again been applied with the horizontal tail surfaces fitted to the aircraft.

○ Two of the wing-mounted ammunition tanks also had a very similar (almost new) sprayed olive green paint finish under the blue topcoat.

The first and most obvious solution was to assume that the tailplanes were changed in service, perhaps having been damaged. This theory is believable, and may well be the case. We knew that the aircraft had been involved in a minor flight-deck accident, but it had sustained no known

Beneath the dark blue paint on the elevator are the remains of the US Navy, three-tone blue and white paint scheme. The stencilled numbers are not fully readable, but are believed to relate to a paint finish/application code. Research to try to link the number sequence to one of the three possible factory production lines, Vought, Brewster or Goodyear, continues. *(FAAM)*

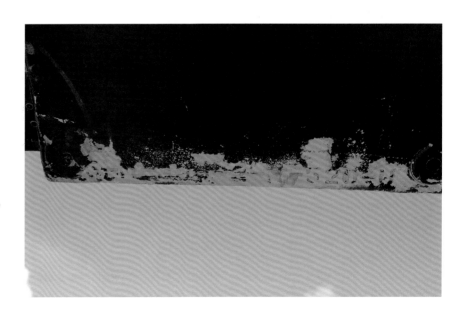

damage to the tail area during this incident. Had another, more major accident required KD431 to have a complete tailplane change? Without the aircraft's complete engineering log book it was very difficult to be sure, but certain pieces of evidence do not point readily towards this.

None of the seven former squadron pilots remember such an incident, bearing in mind that the aircraft was only attached to two squadrons for less than twelve months in total. Their memories of major accident details are usually good when focused on a short period of time with the same aircraft (even aircraft that they were not flying themselves).

No record card or log of such an incident exists, either listing KD431 as having had an independent accident, or as having been in collision with another aircraft.

The modification changes plate has not been stamped to indicate a modification or change.

A more minor incident should not have necessitated the replacement of both tailplanes; this would have defeated the object of the independent replacement system.

There was a lack of witness marks or signs of damage repair in this area of the fuselage, if both tailplanes needed changing. If damage had necessitated the replacement of both horizontal surfaces, why was there no damage to the surrounding components?

Neither the fin nor the relatively delicate rudder showed any signs of having been damaged, repaired or changed. The fuselage sidewalls and

The temperate (olive green, slate grey and duck egg) camouflage, showing through from beneath the wind/air-eroded dark blue top coat, gives every indication of having been factory applied. If this tail unit was transferred in service from another previously flown, earlier aircraft, why is the green finish not also air/wind-eroded? (FAAM)

aluminium skin similarly have no dents, deflections, wrinkling or any other deformation marks that would have resulted from a fairly major accident.

The inside of the tail section box (into which the tailwheel retracts when stowed) also shows no signs of paint flaking or metalwork deformation as the result of an accident or major component removal.

Finally, the most vulnerable component of the whole tail, the thin-walled tail tip cone (which appears to be original to this aircraft) has suffered no major damage or repair.

The only damage that has occurred in this area is some deformation of the tail undercarriage doors. This has been proved to have occurred during the transportation of the aircraft from Cranfield College to Yeovilton in 1963.

The blue paint finish on the tailplane leading edges has been eroded in flight exposing the green camouflage finish beneath. This erosion is normal, and can be seen to a lesser extent in the colour slide showing the aircraft at Cranfield College in 1954 (paint erosion is also evident on the wing leading edges). Further flaking of the blue paint in this eroded area had taken place either at Cranfield or during display at the FAAM.

It is significant that the exposed green camouflage finish shows no signs of erosion and appears to be in very good (almost new) condition, with no chips, erosion wear marks or the like. If these tail surfaces had been previously fitted to another in-service aircraft (and they could only have been fitted to an earlier Brewster-built Corsair Mk III or an early Vought-built example), why are there no witness marks? Moreover, such a removal and substitution would normally be from an older, surplus or damaged aircraft that would probably have had considerable air time and would have developed such erosion marks in this area. (The more recent blue paint on the wing and tailplane leading edges had been eroded quite extensively in only a few months.) The donor aircraft, if there was one, would have had to be in nearly new condition for the temperate finish to be in such good condition. Furthermore, the blue paint finish appears also to have been factory applied.

Also to be considered were the two ammunition tanks with the very-good-condition green paint beneath the blue finish. The same applies to these items. On an active front-line fighting squadron many substitutions of components might have taken place, each leaving the wear and witness marks of such activities. However, the tanks fitted to KD431 seemed to bear no such wear marks or scratches in the original green finish, and had been carefully resprayed and marked in the newer blue finish. Also, as previously mentioned, the coloured pencil/crayon markings (apparently factory references) on the green- and blue-finished tanks match in handwriting style. Was it pure coincidence that KD431 ended up with good-condition green-camouflaged components (overpainted blue) fitted to two different areas of the aircraft but from different sources?

However, there is another interesting possibility. These items might have been fitted at the Goodyear factory. As Goodyear made no green-camouflaged Corsairs, the components could only have originated from one of two other sources: the Vought factory or the Brewster factory.

It does not seem logical that older/earlier batches of temperate-camouflaged Vought parts were redistributed to the Goodyear factory for fitting to its aircraft. Vought was still producing Corsairs at a phenomenal rate, and would have needed every available component to support this level of production. Moreover, KD431's tail surfaces had been sprayed in the temperate scheme while fitted to an aircraft. Why would Vought have removed them from an aircraft and sent them to Goodyear? It just does not make sense.

Focus therefore turns to the Brewster connection. Although it may seem of little importance on the face of it, as no complete Brewster-built Corsairs exist today, it would be important and significant if we were able to prove a link with aircraft produced by that company. Even if Goodyear was receiving pre-sprayed tail components from an external source, it would not have been ordering them pre-sprayed in green camouflage, knowing that it was gearing-up to produce overall blue aircraft. Neither would these parts have been previously fitted to an aircraft unless, of course, that aircraft (or a large subassembly) was in a part-finished state on the terminated Brewster production line.

Research shows that the troubled Brewster Corporation was closed by US government and Navy officials at the end of June 1944. It would be interesting to know conclusively if any part-finished Corsairs, major subassemblies or inventories of parts existed at the Brewster factory at this

An overhead view of the exposed temperate camouflage paint scheme showing through the dark blue top coat. Whatever its origin, this paint, having been concealed from daylight for over half a century, now provides an excellent primary-source colour reference for the Second World War temperate colour scheme of olive green, slate grey and sky ('duck egg') applied to British aircraft. *(FAAM)*

closure date. It is common knowledge that many Brewster aircraft components were scrapped due to poor quality, but it is difficult to believe that any surplus or reclaimable Corsair components were not evaluated (by the government inspectors) and sent to Goodyear for incorporation in their aircraft production.

The inspection tags on the cockpit CO2 bottles appear to put KD431 on the Goodyear production line at around the middle of July 1944, ten to fourteen days after the Brewster factory closure. Most, if not all, of the Brewster-contract Corsairs in production immediately before the closure were for British orders. It is therefore not unreasonable to consider the possibility that Brewster-built British-contract components and/or subassemblies might have been incorporated in British-contract Corsairs on the Goodyear assembly line. No firm evidence has yet been found to prove this; all we can do is examine such evidence that we have and explore the theories.

Further evidence to support this theory came in the form of a chance find in the Goodyear archives. One of the archive's few photographs depicting British Corsair production at the Goodyear plant is an image of Corsair build number 1601. The photograph carries no caption or title, but is dated June 1944. However, the details and evidence within this one picture proved extremely significant to our research and findings.

Corsair fabrication number 1601 relates to British aircraft serial number KD161, the first Corsair manufactured by Goodyear for the British contract. This would be a nice picture to have for a book about FAA Corsairs, but the interest stretches further than that. Firstly, KD161 was delivered to the FAA in July 1944, so the photograph date of June 1944 (showing the aircraft nearly complete) is entirely accurate.

The next point is that, although the aircraft is mostly in primer finish, it is being fitted with numerous components pre-finished in dark glossy blue and, more significantly, in temperate grey/green camouflage. Both outer wing sections are in temperate camouflage, though the starboard wing appears to have an all-blue aileron. Close examination also shows that the elevator and cockpit canopy frames have been finished in dark blue.

Just visible on the extreme right of the picture is the rear fuselage of the next Corsair on the production line. This, presumably, was fabrication number 1602/KD162. (If 1601 was the first British Corsair, with aircraft positioned in front of it, then the production line must travel in reverse, as per the production line photograph shown earlier in this book.) This next Corsair in line clearly has a pre-finished temperate-camouflaged tailplane fitted to a primed fuselage.

A chance find in the Goodyear archive was this study of Goodyear Corsair build number 1601 (KD161), the first British-specification Corsair to roll off the Goodyear production line in July 1944. What a significant picture it is. The elevators, canopy frame, rudder base fillet and starboard aileron are fitted to the chromate-primer-coated fuselage, having been already pre-finished in dark blue. However, both wings are clearly pre-finished in the temperate camouflage scheme. This is proof beyond doubt that temperate-camouflaged components were being fitted to early Goodyear-built British Corsairs, but where did they come from? Just visible at the right-hand edge of the picture is the tail of the next aircraft in line, presumably build number 1602. It has a temperate-scheme elevator fitted to its as yet unfinished primer-coated fuselage. If 1601 is at the head of the production line, then the line must indeed be travelling through the factory backwards. *(Goodyear Tire & Rubber)*

This proves beyond doubt that Goodyear *was* fitting components pre-finished in temperate camouflage to its British-contract aircraft on the assembly line. However, the origin of these parts is unknown; were they ex-Brewster components?

The date of the photograph, June 1944, provides a further clue. This was the month that the troubled Brewster factory was finally closed down by the US government. If Goodyear was to have British Corsairs ready for a July delivery (i.e. actually under construction during June), it would need to be sourcing a steady supply of British-specification components from somewhere. So, with one major production line closing down and another (also government controlled) starting up, the theory becomes more plausible.

Goodyear could not be using up its own old stocks of parts, as any previously built Corsairs on its production line would have been for the US Navy, in US Navy colour scheme (not temperate camouflage), and would not have had the British-specification cropped wingtip.

June 1944 was also two months past the date by which all US Navy aircraft were to be produced in overall glossy sea blue finish (including those built to British contract). It seems very unlikely that, for a brand new production run of all-glossy-blue Corsairs for the British contract, Goodyear would make such an expensive error, in terms of labour and material cost, as to order wings and other components in temperate and not blue from an outside supplier.

However, during June 1944 the failing Brewster factory was trying to produce a final batch of Corsair Mk IIIs to British-contract specification, in temperate-camouflage finish. This raises the question of what happened to any part-finished components and subassemblies from this factory, and whether the government, during a time of war and material shortage, would simply scrap these items when another production line was in the throes of starting up.

Remember that the parent Vought Company also produced temperate-camouflaged Corsairs to British contract. However, research shows that the last British deliveries in temperate scheme from Vought were in 1943. Moreover, with Vought still engaged in full-scale Corsair production, why would it need to redirect components to Goodyear, rather than simply absorbing them into its own production line?

Briggs Industries was obviously being used as an external contract source to provide wings built to British specification, but would not have been supplying Goodyear with temperate-finished wings in June 1944 for a British contract requiring glossy-sea-blue wings. Furthermore, KD431's ammunition tanks and tail surfaces were not Briggs-produced components.

Nor should it be forgotten that the KD431's tailplane was definitely sprayed in its green camouflage finish while fitted to an aircraft (though the aircraft's identity and location are unknown) and then refinished in dark blue at a later stage.

Although conclusive proof is lacking, the evidence strongly suggests that ex-Brewster components and subassemblies might well have been incorporated in KD431 and other early-batch Corsairs on the Goodyear production line.

CRANFIELD CONNECTIONS

In May 1946 Corsair KD431 was officially transferred from the disposals holding yard at Donibristle in Scotland to Cranfield College of Aeronautics, Bedfordshire. The college had strong links with both the RAF and FAA, and many aircraft types were transferred there for engineering training purposes. At that time the college required an up-to-date aircraft with power-folding wings, for the students to use as a study aid. Surviving official correspondence between the college and the Admiralty disposal board shows that KD431 was viewed by college lecturers at Donibristle with this purpose in mind. The official transfer took place in April 1946, and the aircraft arrived at Cranfield in May. It remained there until 1963, when it journeyed to Yeovilton for the opening of the FAAM, where it was one of the first exhibits.

It was essential to find out what had happened to the aircraft during this seventeen-year period, to enable any changes in its appearance or structure to be assessed. Finding people connected with the college (or the aircraft) during this period was still proving difficult, but a small number of former lecturers and college staff were contacted and some useful information surfaced as a result.

Unfortunately the college archives held very little in respect of photographs of the aircraft, most of the useful ones coming from individuals' personal collections. Certain facts, however, were established regarding the aircraft during its time at Cranfield.

Firstly, it was never flown, nor its engine started and run, during this period. The fabric from the starboard wing and elevator were removed to enable the students to study internal mechanical components. The wings themselves were folded and spread to demonstrate the mechanics of such an operation to the students. The power for such an operation would normally have been provided by the hydraulic pump driven by the aircraft's engine when running. However, to enable the college to perform this task more conveniently (and safely) a remote hydraulic rig was attached to the port side of the aircraft. This can clearly be seen in several of the photographs from Cranfield. Fitting this pump necessitated the removal of the port accessory drive access panel, which appears to have been discarded sometime during the Corsair's stay at the college.

The few useful photographs that did emerge from personal albums covered a broad period of time. The earliest currently available shows the aircraft inside one of the hangars at Cranfield, and dates from 1954. The latest shows the aircraft outside the hangars in 1963, awaiting collection by the Royal Navy Aircraft Moving Unit for transportation to Yeovilton.

At this point it is appropriate to note that the actions of the very-far-sighted (and newly formed) Historic Aircraft Preservation Society (HAPS) initiated the saving of the aircraft and its subsequent transfer to the FAAM. Without the intervention of such individuals as Bill Fisher and Russ Snadden, KD431 may well have languished in a poorer environment or, worse, succumbed to the scrap-man's hammer. Aircraft preservation was a relatively new concern at this time, and the HAPS saved many historically significant aeronautical artefacts that would have otherwise been lost for ever.

A close study of several other pictures taken between these dates helps to confirm that little changed on the aircraft during this time. At that stage, satisfied with the information I had gleaned from the few former college associates, I would have said that KD431 had a relatively un-eventful existence at Cranfield.

BIZARRE COINCIDENCE

That changed when I was contacted by Mr Charlie Carter, who had heard I was interested in the Corsair that had been at Cranfield. Although he was not connected with the college, he told me that in the early 1960s he had been the local Cranfield village policeman, and enquired if I knew that the Corsair 'had spent a night at the village pub'. He recounted how, in 1963, as an end-of-term college prank, the engineering students had decided to wheel the aircraft down to the village pub. Under cover of darkness the students pushed it by hand down the narrow road to the village and positioned it on the village green, outside the Swan public house. The following morning, when Mr Carter awoke to prepare for his village policeman's daily duties, he was greeted by the sight of an aircraft on the village green.

Village policeman Charlie Carter 'gets stuck in' to help rescue Corsair KD431 from outside the village public house at Cranfield in 1963. Carter did not realise until 2002 that he had worked on KD431 while serving as an FAA air fitter on HMS *Premier* in 1945. *(C. Carter)*

He recalls that the event caused much amusement throughout the village, and when the college engineering staff arrived with a tow tractor to recover the aircraft, things seemed to go from bad to worse. First, the tractor stalled and proved difficult to restart. Then, when it was finally under way and heading back to the college, the recovery crew managed to snag the port tailplane tip on a telegraph pole strainer wire, causing minor damage to the tip. High jinks and embarrassments over, the aircraft was finally returned to the college. A good story had been shared, and the reason for the minor tailplane repair accounted for, but what followed was quite extraordinary.

Just before Mr Carter finished our very enjoyable telephone conversation, he revealed, almost as an afterthought, that before his police force career he too had served in the FAA. I was interested to know where and when, but Mr Carter dismissed it lightly, saying he had only served for a few months at the end of the Second World War. He said he had been an airfitter on the aircraft carrier HMS *Premier*. I immediately pressed him for more details. The dates and location were remarkable. He had been embarked on *Premier* at the same time as KD431, some seventeen years earlier. As an airfitter he had doubtless worked on the very aircraft that he had rescued from his own village green, and had not even made the connection himself until our conversation nearly sixty years later.

FG-1A OR FG-1D?

A great deal of confusion seems to exist regarding what details distinguish an FG-1A Corsair from an FG-1D, and from which date either type originated. Many books and reference sources seem to vary and conflict. What one would assume to be easily established dates and details are indeed difficult to pinpoint. To be fair, few if any originators of such material had the benefit and luxury of an original Corsair to study while preparing their information, and they could only act on the best information available to them at the time.

Our research explored a great many sources, and it became evident that no single source or document was going to provide conclusive evidence (nothing new about that). It is hoped that this book will update and add to this information, using evidence, facts, fair comparison and physical evidence on the aircraft itself.

Corsairs are often attributed with the A or D type letter codes depending on their technical features. As mentioned elsewhere, the semi-blown canopy hood and single-pylon bomb arrangement are usually regarded as distinguishing features of the FG-1A, whereas the full-blown hood, water-injected 8W-type engine and twin bomb pylons are taken to be FG-1D features.

Looking at all evidence, using the few date references available and comparing all of this against the object itself, we have hopefully fine-tuned this matter. Of all the source documents available, the one we chose as our baseline reference was the Goodyear Aircraft Company log for all Corsairs built by the company: log reference GER-2569.

			LOG: GAC FABRICATION NUMBERS VS BuAER SERIAL NUMBERS FG-I, FG-4 AND F2G AIRPLANES				
GAC FABRICATION NUMBER	BUAER SERIAL NUMBER	BUAER MODEL	CONTRACT NUMBER	NUMBER REQUIRED PER CONTRACT	NUMBER DELIVERED		ALLOCATION
1 thru 299	12992 thru 13290	FG-1	NOa(s) 1871	299	299		United States Navy
300 thru 479	13291 thru 13470	FG-1A	NOa(s) 1871	180 179	180 179		United States Navy GAC #383 PULLED FROM ASSY LINE FOR DUMMY CARBURETOR INTAKE TEST & INCREASED NOSE WEIGHT TO SIMULATE THE 4360 ENGINE.
480 and 481	13471 and 13472	XF2G-1	NOa(s) 1871	2	2		United States Navy - assigned to Goodyear Aircraft Corporation Experimental
482 thru 1600	13473 thru 14591	FG-1A	NOa(s) 1871	1119 1117	1119 1117		United States Navy GAC #1100 & 1101 PULLED FROM ASSY LINE FOR TEST WITH BUBBLE CANOPY.
1601 thru 1699	14592 thru 14690	FG-1A	NOa(s) 1871	99	99		United Kingdom - KD161 thru KD259
1700 thru 1704	14691 thru 14695	XF2G-1	NOa(s) 1871	5	5		United States Navy - assigned to Goodyear Aircraft Corporation Experimental
1705 thru 2000	14696 thru 14991	FG-1A	NOa(s) 1871	296	296		United Kingdom - KD265 thru KD560
2001 thru 2307	76139 thru 76445	FG-1D	NOa(s) 1871 Addition No. 1	306	306		United Kingdom - KD561 thru KD867

The Goodyear aircraft factory fabrication log. Without this official numbering record, the extraordinary numerical coincidences concerning KD431 might never have been noticed. *(Goodyear Tire & Rubber)*

I am convinced in my own mind that there are indeed minor discrepancies in this document. These typically relate to small numbers of aircraft being diverted for trials, incompleted batches, or returns to the production line, as was the case with most aircraft production plants. However, Goodyear produced the aircraft and Goodyear produced this document, so its accuracy has to be regarded as sound as any.

Some key facts provide a basis for a more detailed analysis of KD431's build date and type:

- Most source documents regard April 1943 as the first production month for Goodyear-built Corsairs.

- By March 1944 the 1,000th Goodyear Corsair had been produced.

- April 1944 is recognised as being the point of change to the overall blue colour schemes.

- July 1944 saw the first batch of Goodyear Corsairs delivered to the Royal Navy, starting with KD161 (build number 1601).

- September 1944 is widely regarded as the date from which FG-1Ds were produced, incorporating the new canopy, twin pylons and 8W water-

injection engine. This took place from aircraft Bureau number
76139/fabrication number 2001/serial number KD561 onwards.

○ Most of the technical details on KD431 point clearly to the aircraft being
an FG-1A.

The aircraft is based on a centre section that has the single centrally
mounted bomb rack. Internally, this centre section has no castings,
brackets or other associated provision for the twin pylon mounts that
came with the later D-type aircraft. The outer wings do not have (and
have no provision for) the externally mounted rocket rails, another feature
regarded as specific to D-type aircraft, and the cockpit canopy is of the
semi-blown type, correct for the FG-1A.

However KD431 has the 8-W-type engine that is widely regarded as
being specific to D-type aircraft, and this was clearly installed in the
factory. So when was the 8-W engine introduced, and was it factory fitted
to FG-1A Corsairs?

Certainly the Pratt & Whitney R2800 10-W variant was being made
available to the Grumman Aircraft Company from as early as February

*The Goodyear factory test pilots
line up for a photograph in
1944. Chris Clarke, the first man
to fly KD431, is third in line (in
uniform) from the left. (Goodyear
Tire & Rubber)*

1944, for installation in the company's Hellcat fighter. This engine, also water-injected, differed only from the 8W in that its rear accessory drive case was turned through 180 degrees to accommodate the Hellcat's particular carburettor arrangement. Otherwise it can be likened to the 8W type. It seems reasonable that Pratt & Whitney could have been supplying other users of this fully developed production engine at or around this time. Pinning a build date to KD431 would help to clarify this.

Starting at fabrication number 2001 (the first FG-1D) and calculating back to fabrication number 1871 (KD431), it can be seen that the FAAM's aircraft was 129 places ahead of the first D-type aircraft in the production line. The absence of the manufacturer's cockpit plate, which would give date, aircraft model and engine number, leaves little physical evidence of an exact build date for KD431. However, we can accurately place KD431 within the month of July 1944 by other means. The high-pressure CO_2 cockpit bottle is dated July 1944. This may well offer an accurate date for the aircraft, but are the labels accurate to the production-line date, or substituted from other bottles, fitted at a different time? Accurate details as to how the factory dealt with the daily completion of aircraft would doubtless help in this area of research.

At this point I was fortunate to be able to locate and talk to Mr Chris Clark, now living in Kansas City, USA. Not only was Mr Clark a former Goodyear test pilot, but he was also the very first person to fly KD431, on 22 August 1944. Information gleaned from Mr Clark was to prove vital to our research in this aspect of the aircraft's history.

The following extracts are from conversations with Mr Clark regarding this specific area of his career and time at the Goodyear factory:

I was at Goodyear from November 1, 1943, until September 1, 1944.

There were twenty test pilots on strength at that time, if you include the senior and second senior test pilots. However, these two did not fly every day, and so I suppose it would be more accurate to say that there would have been eighteen regular flyers.

Flying would normally take place between the hours of eight in the morning and five in the afternoon. This was dependent on weather conditions and the time of year. All of our test flights had to be made in good clear conditions and with good visibility.

If we were behind a little on schedules or if the weather was particularly good, they may have opened the airfield a little earlier for flying, or on a particularly fine afternoon you may have got a five o'clock flight, but normally eight-to-five flying.

Typically you would get one flight per day, maybe two at very best. There would be at least one hour of pre-flight checks, which would then have to be written-up as two or three pages of notes.

Then of course you could begin your test flight. All Navy Corsairs at Goodyear had to undergo two hours of test flying. You would take the aircraft up for maybe twenty or thirty minutes, maybe more, making notes in flight on how the aircraft was performing and handling, listening for strange noises, that sort of thing.

Then you would land back on the airfield and write these notes up so that you could pass the information to the flight rectification centre. Here they would rectify the reported defects and then you would be able to complete the flight programme for that aircraft. Of course, depending on the nature of the fault, this could be hours or days apart.

The second test flight would then total the remainder of the two-hour slot, or as near to as possible.

Corsair production in 1944 was around eight aircraft per day on average, so it would be safe to say that we were turning out around 240–50 aircraft per month. From memory, an aircraft's components would take about one month to produce, then when it had started to be assembled on the production line it was on the line for about one week.

When it had left the line and been painted it would go to the pre-flight preparation line. Here it would have all the systems checked, fluids topped up, engine started and test run for a specified time and any fine adjustments made. An aircraft could be here for two days easily.

Then out to the flight park to await its turn for a test flight. This, as mentioned, was dependent on weather, time of flight, any problems and the time it took to fix them. Then the aircraft could be assigned to the park of aircraft waiting to be ferried to the delivery point. We took a lot of our Corsairs to Newark Airport in New York. You could land at the airport and then the aircraft could be taken across the road, directly into the harbour dock area for loading on to ships. We took a lot of our aircraft this route.

This information was invaluable. We now knew that an aircraft was on the production line for approximately one week. It was then finish-painted (other sources indicate approximately two days plus for this operation, including markings). Then a minimum of two days was spent in the

The flight log book entry for Goodyear test pilot Chris Clark shows that KD431 made its first flight on 22 August 1944. A second, sign-off flight was made two days later after adjustments and rectification of minor faults. *(C. Clark)*

pre-flight preparation line. The aircraft was then parked in line, awaiting
its turn for test flight among many dozens of other completed aircraft, at a
turn-around rate of twenty or so per day, if all eighteen pilots were able to
fly with no problems. This gave an average minimum (combined) production and standing time per aircraft of around fifteen days.

Combining this information with other known figures enabled us to
begin to define more accurately the build date and specification of KD431.
Build number 1871 is 871 places further on in production from Corsair
build number 1000 of March 1944. If we took the date tag attached to
KD431's cockpit CO_2 bottle as a possible reference to the aircraft's production date of somewhere in the middle of July 1944, did the sums work?

A total of 871 aircraft built between March and mid-July (3½ months),
gives an average of 248.8 aircraft per month. This agrees with Mr Clark's
figure of 240–50 aircraft per month, and would therefore put the start-of-
build date of aircraft build number 1871 (KD431) somewhere between the
middle and end of July 1944. Adding the fifteen days (minimum)
combined production, commissioning and standing time to this puts the
first test flight for KD431 at somewhere around the middle of August,
plus or minus a few days.

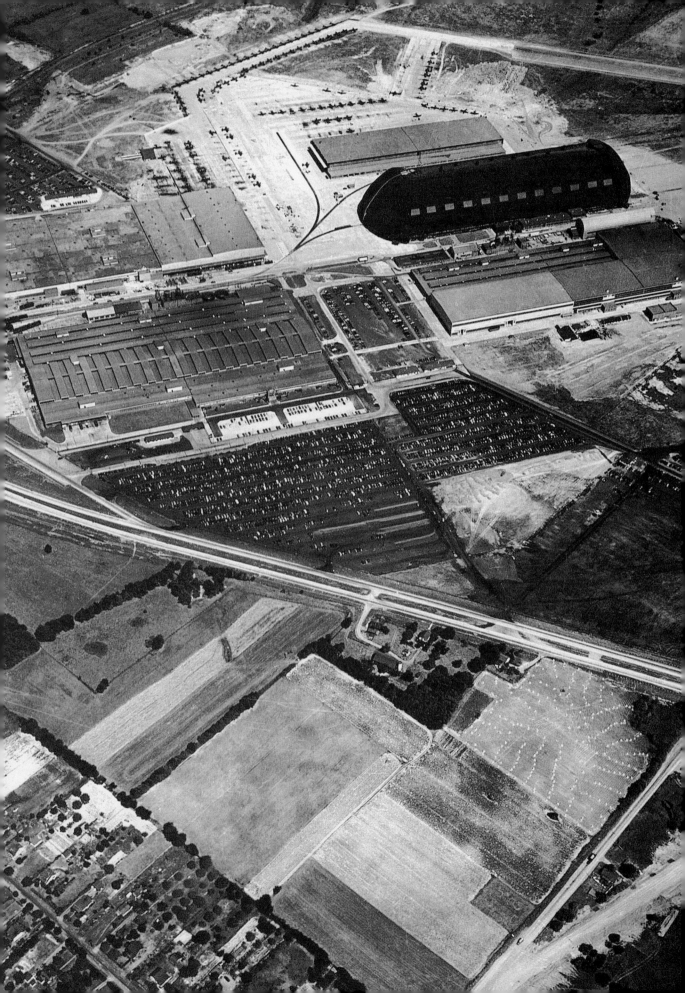

Project completed. The 'time capsule'; imagine you were able to reach into history and pick out an aircraft at random as a type example and object of study. Corsair KD431 is now as close as possible to being just that. The date is 2004, but what you see, after four years of painstaking work, is 1944. *(FAAM)*

This is a rough guide, and there are no accurate details of production-line speed or delays, or daily variances in post-production-line standing time, but in broad terms the sums appear to work. It is known that KD431 was first flown on 22 August 1944. The actual assembly start date for the aircraft may never be known, but the CO_2 bottle inspection tag date of 10 July 1944 appears to provide an accurate reference to when components were being assembled on to this aircraft on the production line.

When all of the previous evidence is combined with these findings, it appears that model 8W engines were being fitted to Corsairs as early as July 1944 and, unless KD431 was the first to receive this engine, it must be assumed that earlier aircraft were similarly equipped.

VARIOUS STAGES OF KD431 REVEALED DURING THE PROJECT

Factory Production Line (Plan View)

Plan view showing KD431 as it would have appeared on the Goodyear production line, after assembly, but before final paint finish of all-over glossy sea blue. Note: in this instance the horizontal tail surfaces were temperate camouflage, elevators finished in US Navy non-spectacular blue and two of the wing-mounted ammunition tanks are in olive green. Many early Goodyear Corsairs for the British contract would have shared similar variations in their production line colour schemes, but where were all of these odd-coloured components coming from?

STAGE 1. Factory production line

This is how KD431 would have looked while on the Goodyear factory production line in July–August 1944. Pre-finished blue components, such as the canopy, undercarriage and wings, would have been fitted to the yellow-chromate primed fuselage as the aircraft travelled along the production line. Note also the pre-finished temperate-camouflage tail components. These might have originated from the Brewster Aircraft Factory, closed in June of that year.

STAGE 2. Factory build complete

With production complete, in August 1944, the aircraft would have been sprayed in glossy sea blue. The basic British insignia would have been applied (roundels, serial number, 'Royal Navy' wording and fin flash), but no other British markings would have been applied at this stage. The code '431' applied to the nose was a temporary application for factory and delivery identification.

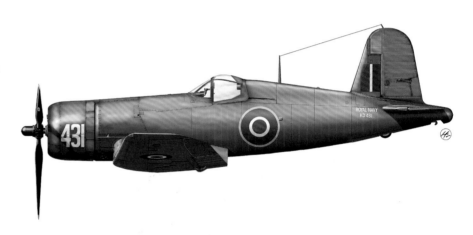

STAGE 3. Delivery to Great Britain

To protect the aircraft from salt water during its transatlantic journey as ship's cargo in November 1944, many areas were protected. The engine compartment and cockpit were protected with fitted canvas covers; the wing-fold, exhausts and air intake areas were shielded with doped fabric strips; and the wheels were spray-coated with a preservative wax. The whole aircraft was then sprayed with a coat of light oil.

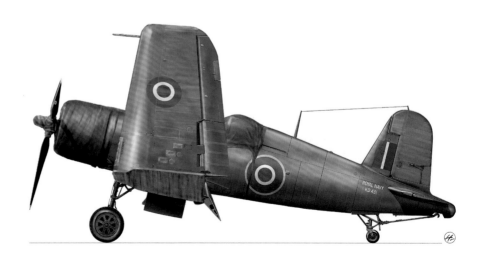

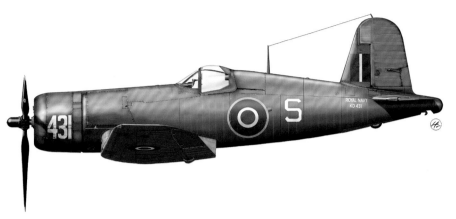

STAGE 4. First squadron

Corsair KD431 was first attached to 1835 Sqn, in January 1945. At this stage it received its first official squadron marking, a single letter 'S' painted in white on the fuselage sides and on the front undercarriage plates, which acted as the individual call-sign code for that aircraft. The factory-applied '431' on the nose of the aircraft would have been left to deteriorate away.

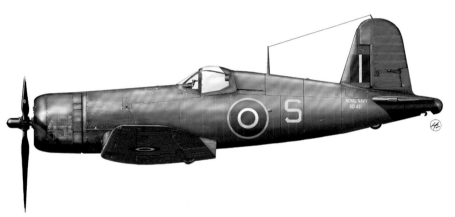

STAGE 5. Preparation for war in the Far East

In July 1945 1835 Sqn was instructed to prepare its aircraft to join other squadrons in the South East Asia Command and Pacific theatres of war. At this stage the code letter 'S' would have been altered to pale blue in accordance with Admiralty instructions. It is believed that the gas-reactive patch discovered on the port wing was also applied at this time. The factory code '431' would have been a lot less obvious at this stage.

STAGE 6. Postwar squadron

The war ended just as 1835 Sqn was preparing to go, in early August 1945, so KD431 did not see action in the Far East. In September 1945 the aircraft was transferred to 768 Sqn, and continued to serve as a deck-landing training aircraft until December of that year. At this stage the 'S' codes were painted over with grey paint (presumably all that was available), and the new 'E2-M' code was applied. In addition, the canopy frame received the yellow emergency-cut lines during this period. By then the factory applied '431' code had all but disappeared owing to oil, grime and erosion. *(FAAM)*

CONCLUSION

Corsair KD431, fabrication number 1871, Bu No. 14862, is without doubt a Model FG-1A, complete with a Pratt & Whitney R2800-8W engine as fitted at the Goodyear factory during July 1944.

The aircraft retains numerous interesting, unique and historically important details, any one of which is noteworthy, and as a whole represents an extremely valuable time capsule. It is:

1. An example of a Second World War aircraft still in largely factory-original condition, including its original factory-applied paintwork, stencils and markings.

2. An example of a Second World War Royal Navy fighter retaining its correct and authentic markings from two 1940s FAA squadrons, with very few changes from its factory-fresh condition.

3. A valuable and possibly unique reference to the exact colours and markings of this period, including accurate and authentic in-the-field modifications.

4. A valuable reference to the exact techniques, materials and applications used during American aircraft production during the Second World War.

5. An aircraft possibly demonstrating a unique link with the Brewster Aircraft company.

It is believed to be the last remaining truly authentic, most complete and original example of a Corsair anywhere in the world. To repaint this aircraft, start the engine, fly it, or alter it in any way would be a crime that could not be redressed. This is the last one left.

Chapter Six

Corsair Pilots Speak

Perhaps it is the Corsair's ability to create extreme reactions that helps to make it such a favourite. Some see it as an embodiment of grace and beauty, others as a brutish killing machine, or even a combination of the two. But what did it mean to those who took the reins of this awesome creature and tried to tame it, the men who flew the mighty Corsair?

The following extracts come from conversations with former pilots who trained on Corsairs and flew them on 1835 and 768 Sqns, FAA, during the Second World War, and also from Lt Cdr Donald MacQueen, who trained hundreds of new pilots in the art of deck-landing the Corsair. Their memories are vivid and their fondness for the aeroplane is obvious, but their experiences clearly demonstrate how learning to fly the Corsair could be as dangerous as real combat.

LT CDR DONALD MACQUEEN, DECK LANDING AND TRAINING INSTRUCTOR (NORTH AMERICA)

'Each pilot would have to do at least 150 ADDLS before I would even consider them to be capable of a true deck landing.'

Donald MacQueen was posted to North America as a pilot attached to No. 845 NAS, primarily to assist in training pilots on Grumman Avengers. During this time his ability to signal/direct aircraft on to the airfield dummy deck-landing area (using bats) developed, and his potential was recognised. Soon he was removed from pilot training and flying to assist full time with this task. With the arrival of the new Corsair squadrons MacQueen was swiftly presented with the challenge of training these new pilots to land the Corsair safely on a carrier flight deck. His new title (a one-off to suit this unique position) was Deck Landing and Training Instructor North America. In effect he was now responsible for training all new British pilots posted to North America for pilot training in the recognised method of safe approach to an aircraft carrier. This required

Lt Cdr Donald MacQueen, right.
(The National Archive, USA)

The initial land-based training
flights for flight-deck landings
were known as Airfield Dummy
Deck Landings, or ADDLs. An
area of runway was marked out
to resemble the size and layout
of a carrier's flight deck, and
pilots were trained to bring an
aircraft into land on this defined
patch by following the
batsman's signals. Only when
the batsman was satisfied with a
pilot's consistent approach to
this 'land-deck' would a
shipboard deck landing be
attempted. *(FAAM)*

the following of a recognised code of hand signals relayed by highly visible coloured bats held (one in each hand) by the training instructor (batsman). The US Navy used a similar system, but it worked in exactly the opposite way to the British method. There was evidently room for serious error; hence the necessity for a deck-landing control officer to suit the Royal Navy's training needs.

The American system was to indicate to the incoming pilot how his aircraft was positioned in relation to the ship (high, low, angle, and so on), leaving the pilot to work out the necessary corrections for himself. The British method was for the batsman to indicate to the pilot what he needed to do to correct his approach. Each method worked well, provided the pilot was familiar with the appropriate discipline. However, a moment's lapse in concentration by either pilot or batsman, or a pilot's reluctance to trust the batsman's every instruction, could lead to disaster, possibly with fatal consequences.

A take-off in a Corsair could be equally hazardous. An inadvertent touch of the brakes or a little too much elevator input could soon remind a pilot of the close proximity of propeller and deck. (The National Archive, USA)

I had done some 'batting on' before I was posted to America, so I suppose I had a feel for it. I was meant to be in America for Avenger pilot training and torpedo instruction, but they noticed that I had an eye for batting aircraft on to the deck. Of course I had to get familiar with the Corsair myself first, and then start putting the students through the rigorous programme of Airfield Dummy Deck Landings (ADDLS). I would train them in groups of four. Each pilot would have to do at least 150 ADDLS before I would even consider them to be capable of a true deck landing. A few were ready before this, but most took at least 150 landings. I could very often tell after a while who was who in the circuit or on the approach. Many of the pilots had their own tell-tale signs in flight that I could recognise.

Then every two or three weeks we would go down to Chesapeake Bay and complete training with four actual deck landings on USS *Charger*. [An American-built carrier originally destined for the Royal Navy but retained in the USA as a training carrier for both the US and British Services.] Landing on a carrier, of course, was a lot more dangerous. If you got it wrong on the airfield it could be bad enough, but on a carrier there was no room for error. If you overshot or swung on landing you would be into the barrier or over the side of the ship. I had two 'tellers' to help me on the deck, there was simply not time to watch out for everything. One would watch the aircraft that had landed and tell me if it was clear of the arrester wires or was having any problems. Sometimes I could catch a glimpse of what was going on behind me, but really once I had got one aircraft on to the deck that was no longer my business, unless I had a clear signal from one of the tellers that there was a problem. I had to focus on the next incoming aircraft and make a decision within 20–30 seconds if it was safe to bring him in to land. The other 'teller' would be using binoculars, watching the next aircraft on approach. This was to check, further out than I could see with my own eyes, if the incoming aircraft had any obvious problems; wheels not down, hook not down, that sort of thing. There were, of course, many accidents when the aircraft was actually on the deck. Such as missing the wires, charging the barrier or, worse, jumping the barrier or going over the side of the ship, but I can say that I only lost one aircraft on approach to the ship.

During his career as a Royal Navy batsman and Flight Deck Officer, Lt Cdr MacQueen can probably claim title to having 'batted on' more Navy pilots than any other batsman in the Service, probably in excess of 150,000 landings in this period alone (approximately 1,000 trainee pilots at 150 ADDLs each, followed by at least four full ship's deck landings per pilot). Hundreds of FAA pilots quite literally owe their life to the skill, judgement and patience of Donald MacQueen.

Brewster-built Corsair '7Y', serial number JS615, skipped the crash barrier on landing. Donald MacQueen remembers this event well. 'The aircraft skipped the barrier and ended up on its nose, balanced precariously between the propeller blades and a wingtip. They had to keep the ship steering just enough into wind to prevent the aircraft from toppling over while safety lines were attached. The poor pilot had many nerve-racking minutes in his lofty perch until the safety crews could rescue him. At any moment the aircraft could have fallen on to its back with disastrous consequences. His rescue was a marvellous piece of teamwork between the ship's crew and the flight-deck recovery crew.' *(The National Archive, USA)*

Stan Deeley, 1835 Sqn. *(FAAM)*

STAN DEELEY, No. 1835 NAS

'I loved the Corsair, a wonderful aeroplane.'

We did all our basic training in America at various airfields; Brunswick, Pensacola, Corrie Field. We trained first on Boeing Stearmans and then Harvards before getting on to Corsairs. Then came the deck landings. We went down to Norfolk, Virginia, and had to fly on to USS *Charger*. You had to complete four good deck landings to pass the test. You would land on the ship and hopefully take a wire [arrester wire], and then be unhooked and pushed backwards to the rear of the flight deck by the deck handling crew. All this with the engine still running, very dangerous. Then you would take off and go around again, three more times.

If you were successful a man would come on to the deck holding a large board that read: YOU HAVE QUALIFIED – RETURN TO BASE. It reminded me of the clapperboard man in the movies.

We had to follow the batsman's signals to get on to the ship. Batting was opposite to the Americans. Their version was to show you what you were already doing, leaving you to make judgements and corrections for yourself. The British method was to show you what to do, i.e. guide you in safely to the ship, correcting and helping you all the way in. Donald [MacQueen] would tell you what to do; he would get you down.

We were all supposed to do one night-time deck take-off and landing. I remember we were all ranged on the flight deck at night, engines running, waiting to be marshalled into position for take-off. We were all parked very tight at the rear of the ship. Suddenly there was a lot of clattering, and I noticed that my starboard wing was being hit by another propeller. Immediately I selected wing fold and cut the engine, but the damage was done. Someone had removed my chocks without giving me the signal, and I was not fully on the brakes. I had then crept forward into the next aircraft. Commander Flying [FlyCo] sent for me immediately, to explain what had happened. He was so incensed with rage that he took off his officer's cap and jumped on it. I got a severe dressing-down over that incident.

Gunnery practice was shooting at a towed banner in flight. Another aircraft would tow a banner or drogue behind them on a very long cable. We had to approach from different angles and fire at the drogue. The guns were ranged so that the bullets filled a target circle of approximately 6ft in diameter at 300yd. The bullets would be coated in a semi-dry coloured paint that would leave a clear indication of who had hit the target. We each had a different colour, of course. We only had two guns armed for target shooting, the Corsair cannon were so powerful we would have destroyed the target with all six. A ten per cent hit rate was considered quite good in target shooting.

Safely down, exactly central and picking up the fifth wire, Corsair '875' makes a textbook landing. Note the aircraft's wingspan in relation to the width of the flight deck. There was little or no room for error on the narrow decks of British aircraft carriers. *(FAAM)*

We did a lot of simulated combat training. Turning in tight circles, trying to out-turn each other and get behind the other aircraft. It was very difficult to keep turning tight, the aircraft would judder and be right on the point of stalling. Always turning tight, no fancy aerobatics like you see in films. Following an aircraft in aerobatics is quite easy, following in a tight turn and trying to out-turn each other is much more difficult.

Aerobatics in general were forbidden, although we did do them; we were young!

Once I tried a snap roll in the Corsair and nearly didn't come out of it. The violence of the manoeuvre was very frightening. I remember the control stick came right back into the corner of the cockpit and I had to use both hands to force it back into the middle and regain control. Thankfully I had enough height or I would have been a goner.

Low flying was also restricted to certain areas, although this wasn't always followed.

I remember low flying one winter afternoon in a forbidden area with John Taylor. Typical Maine winter; grey sky, visibility not good. We were flying side-by-side formation and broke left and right. I remember being alarmed to see a large grey shape in front of me. This rapidly turned out to be some large trees in the mist. I tried to pull clear but clattered through some of the branches.

John re-formed on me and said that it looked like I had an oil leak, so I headed for base quickly. The mechanics took a look as soon as I had landed, and said that I only had about ten minutes of oil left. When I went around to the front of the aircraft and looked, all of the oil coolers were leaking and stuffed full of smashed-up branches. I had been very lucky to get away with that, but now I had to write a report!

I wrote my accurate report and took it to the CO. His name was Tobias Joshua Alphonso King-Joyce; we called him 'Spike' for short. A great character, reputed to have been related to 'Lord Haw-Haw' and to have been a mercenary in General Franco's forces before the war.

Spike took one look at my report and said: 'You hand this in and you are for the high-jump. Go away and re-write it.'

My second report read: 'Practising vertical upward spins, lost control, spun out and went into downward spiral. Recovered in time but collided with trees on high ground.' I received a due telling off and no more was said!

Once I went as high as I could go in a Corsair. I got it to 32,000ft! The last 1,000ft took ages to climb, the aircraft was wallowing around and would not fly very well. Then I thought: 'Oh well, let's see how fast it would dive', so I rolled into a vertical dive from 32,000ft and just went as fast as I could. We were fearless, you just did these things to experiment. I pulled out in good time but was sure that I had seen a colour change happen over the wings as I pulled out of the dive. I can't really explain, it just looked as if the wings had changed colour momentarily. I remember doing the true calculation for the dive speed in the classroom later. Allowing for pilot error, air density, dive angle etc., it came out at 600mph. I don't know if I actually did 600mph, but it was certainly more than the recommended top speed of 400. The change of colour was presumably a condensation layer forming over the wing!

One beautiful moonlit night we were up as a flight of four, line-astern, close formation, with John Morton leading. Just for our own amusement we did some formation aerobatics. John led the formation up into a vertical climb and then a loop, all of us in formation! John, then me second, followed by Jack Sheppard and Bill Plews. I remember I was still on the way up when John passed me on the way down – back-to-back in the moonlight! We did crazy things like that.

JOHN TAYLOR, No. 1835 NAS

'The Corsair. The best seaborne fighter of the whole war. Tough, rugged, took lots of punishment – very manoeuvrable.'

We left Britain headed for Boston on the RMS *Mauritania*. We were escorted until we were clear of the coast of Ireland, and then full steam

John Taylor, 1835 Sqn. *(FAAM)*

A clear study of the arrester hook safely engaged with one of the ship's deck arrester wires. Take-off and landing procedures required the cockpit canopy to be locked in the fully open position to facilitate the pilot's escape if things went wrong. *(FAAM)*

until we reached Boston. I don't think there was much fear of U-boat attacks by then, though.

Our training took us all over the place.

From Boston we went by train to Monkton, New Brunswick, Canada. We were there for three weeks. Then via Montreal to Detroit. Here we flew Boeing Stearman biplanes until we were able to go solo. Then by train again to Pensacola; here we flew Vultee Valiant aircraft. From here we transferred to Corrie Field (near Pensacola) for training on Harvard aircraft. After three months we finally qualified as pilots and were presented with our wings – US Naval Air Corps Wings. Nothing from the Fleet Air Arm. From here we transferred to Jacksonville for Corsair training. I can't tell you what an ominous-looking beast the Corsair was after flying the Harvard.

We began Corsair training by ground taxying with wings folded, just to familiarise ourselves with its size and power. We lost one poor chap, he tried taking off with his wings still folded, nerves I guess, or just a bad mistake. It was all still quite nerve-racking, we were all still so young. He crashed into the trees at the end of the runway; very sad,

very sad. They made a great effort to ensure that we all had our wings spread and locked in place before take-off after that.

Finally we were allowed to take off. We were told to go and find some clear airspace and practise landing on clouds. This was to get us familiar with approaching, handling and pretend landing at a safe height. We finished our flying course at Jacksonville; by then I had completed nearly 600 flying hours flying various aircraft.

You got free periods during training to go off and fly on your own or in small groups, to practise what you had been learning on Corsairs. This is where most of the rule-bending came in. Stan [Stan Deeley] and I decided in one free period to fly our Corsairs from Jacksonville to Tampa and back, just for a flight, just for fun. It must have been a 400-mile round trip. On the way back I was feeling a bit confident, thought I would show off a bit to anyone watching from down below. I tried a slow roll. Big mistake, it just slipped out of the roll. My first reaction was to pull back hard on the stick; this just made things worse. The next thing the wings were juddering and I was approaching a high-speed stall situation. I was very lucky to regain control, very lucky. I didn't do that again – very frightening.

We did what we called overhead gunnery practice, that was firing at a banner being towed by another aircraft. The banner was being towed at 10,000ft, and you would approach from 15,000ft, roll and dive down on to the target inverted. Timing was critical; too late and you would miss the target. Too short and you would hit the towing cable. Inverted, nearly blacking out, concentrating on flying, firing at the banner, not colliding with the tow cable – it scared the Hell out of me.

You took turns flying in the tow aircraft with the gunnery instructor. He would fly the tow plane and talk you through what everyone else was doing right or wrong. You sat in the rear cockpit of the Harvard and watched what was going on. One day I was up with the instructor, we were flying along over the ranges at Jacksonville when the instructor was shot by a stray rifle bullet from the gunnery ranges below. A completely freak accident. He called out that he had been shot and to take the controls. At first I did not believe him, but soon I could see it was for real. We made an emergency landing and they whisked him off to hospital. It was a good job that it was a dual-control Harvard!

From Jacksonville we went to Brunswick, Maine, USA, to form Squadron 1835. Here we started working-up for deck landing with the Corsair; 'Spike' King-Joyce was the squadron CO. We did forbidden, unofficial things, like low flying under bridges, or making mock attacks on US cruisers off the Portland coast. It was all supposed to be forbidden, but we still did it.

From here we went down to Norfolk, Virginia, for deck-landing training on USS *Charger* in Chesapeake Bay. Back to Brunswick, then New York and home on another ocean liner. When we arrived back in Great Britain we went to Eglinton, Northern Ireland, to continue training.

Oh yes, the Corsair, once you had got used to it, it really was a marvellous aeroplane.

JOHN MORTON, No. 1835 NAS

'A very strong, powerful aircraft.'

We all did much the same route in America as I recall, ending up at Brunswick on Corsairs. We did a lot of aerobatics and combat formation training. The Americans were keen to teach us that the best way to lose a Zero was by diving steeply and then a sharp turn to the left. This, of course, led us to experiment with ever-steeper dives and how fast we could go. I remember, you did these dives and, as you became more familiar with the aircraft, of course, your dives became faster and from a greater height.

I remember I was in a very steep dive to see what I could do. I don't know exactly what speed I managed, but it was quite respectable. A lot more than 400mph.

I remember that the first thing to go was the forward aerial mast; it just ripped off. Then a cowling on top of the fuselage between the rear of the engine and the cockpit peeled away. Then the controls went into reversal (ailerons and elevator); this was very frightening. I managed, somehow, to get back in control and decided not to try that again, at least not quite like that. We were pushing the Corsair too far; we were going too far with this diving business.

One chap came back with his Corsair after a steep dive, with the skin on the rear of the fuselage wrinkled. He must have pulled too sharp out of a very steep dive and wrinkled the back of the aircraft between the cockpit and the tail. They called a halt to it after that.

Slow rolls and snap rolls were taught in training. The Americans were keen on it. It was nice in a Stearman, but totally different in a Corsair. I nearly broke both my knees trying a snap roll for the first time in a Corsair. I remember the control column smashed around the inside of the cockpit at an alarming rate. It hit both my knees hard on the insides and I had a couple of good bruises. Quite frightening the speed that it reacted. The aircraft coped all right, but it was quite frightening.

Postwar, while still in Royal Navy service, John Morton extended his flying career by training as a helicopter pilot. After leaving the Service this extremely talented aviator joined the Fairey Aviation Company (later absorbed into Westland Helicopters Ltd), and was involved in the development of many British-built helicopters.

TONY MITCHELL, No. 1835 NAS

'Wonderful aeroplane, wonderful. I simply loved the Corsair.'

We left for Canada after doing our basic training at Gosport, England. This was drill training, not flying training; you know, square-bashing and marching.

We arrived at Monkton, Canada, and then went on to Detroit as trainee pilots.

The first problem a lot of students encountered was airsickness; we had not been tested for airsickness in England. A lot of students had problems with this and were sent home (England). It was remarkable; we had gone all that way to train as pilots and had not been tested for airsickness.

We started training on Stearmans, then Vultee Valiants. Then we progressed to Harvards. Finally at Jacksonville we got our Corsairs. The Corsair was wonderful, such immense power. It looked such a beast. You could soon get into trouble with it, but once you were familiar it was a superb aeroplane.

We formed a squadron back in Maine. Spike King-Joyce was the CO. I expect that you have heard all about him!

Here it was airfield dummy deck landing training, before going to North Virginia for deck landing proper on USS *Charger*. Deck landings were with new Mk IV Corsairs; we picked these up in Maine and flew down to North Virginia.

Lieutenant-Commander Donald MacQueen was sent over to the US as our bats training officer. The British batted aircraft on to carriers opposite to the US method: This caused a lot of problems. We had to have our own bats training. Donald was the only batsman sent over; he must have batted more pilots in than anybody. Every course, every squadron, every day. He did it thousands of times, and he could recognise a lot of us by our approach.

We did a lot of formation flying in Maine. Tight formations and close-following line-astern formations.

Once we were following Spike, the CO, in a long line, six or seven of us. Close follow-my-leader fashion. If he turned, we all turned; if he climbed, we all climbed, following tight. We were out over a big lake and he started to climb straight up. At the top of the climb he would break either left or right and we would have to all follow in turn. I was about third back from Spike, going up in the climb, when the man in front broke early and pulled back. He was right in front and coming directly back on to me. I had to pull back like Hell and hope that I did not hit the man behind me. Somehow we all missed each other, but it left me in an inverted flat spin, at about 10,000ft above the lake.

Onc thing we were all told in training was not to get into any flat spin, let alone inverted. I remember it was a glorious afternoon, and there I was, falling like a leaf. Looking through the top of my cockpit canopy, not upwards but down at the lake, just falling like a leaf in my Corsair, watching the lake coming up at me. I remember thinking: 'Oh well, today must be the day'. Whatever I was doing, I must have done something right with the stick or pedals, and at the last minute the old Corsair rolled itself back upright. I was very low but I managed to pull away safely. That was probably my worst moment.

Back in England we went to Eglinton and did more deck-landing practice on HMS *Premier*, out in the Irish Sea. It was here that I did my first catapult-boosted Corsair launch.

That was a frightening episode. I remember being on the deck, all lined up and ready to go. Engine flat out, one hand on the throttle, the other arm forming a contorted strut between the control stick and your stomach. This was

Close formation flying was an essential element of flying training. This picture shows a very experienced group of trainee Corsair pilots in tight formation, over Maine in the USA. The Corsairs are a mixture of early marks, two of which have the 'birdcage'-type canopy. *(FAAM)*

to help prevent you pulling back too hard on the stick as you were boosted down the deck.

Watching for the Flight Deck Officer to drop the flag. Then suddenly you were off! And I mean suddenly. The next thing that you knew, you were clearing the end of the deck, out over the sea, just coming around from near blackout. You had to think fast, clear your head, check flaps, control the stick, check rudder, engine speed, select undercarriage up, check altitude – check it all again, think clearly and then you were clear of the ship. That went OK, and then you had to get in the circuit and start thinking about a deck landing. Oh yes, that was a pretty hairy experience, I can tell you.

Tony Mitchell was one of the few pilots we traced who actually flew KD431, or 'King-Dog', as he so fondly referred to it, from call-sign terminology.

Despite his failing health Tony made many trips to the FAAM, aiding my research, helping to track down other No. 1835 NAS pilots, providing encouragement for the project or simply enjoying a chat over a cup of tea. His log book entries were key to providing dated proof as to the where-abouts of KD431, and the only photograph of KD431 in service was provided courtesy of Tony's log book/diary.

An impeccably tidy man, I think he found it a little strange that we wanted to return the smart-looking (though incorrectly painted) aircraft that stood in the museum, to a war-worn example. As the project progressed, though, so his view changed, as he began to realise that this was not fake distressing or replicating an aged effect; it was the real thing.

I recall standing with him in the hangar, looking at the now exposed, worn and scratched paintwork from its time in service, and how he remarked: 'I must have clambered up the side of that aeroplane countless times nearly sixty years ago. I must even have made some of those marks and scratches. Who would have thought that it would still exist, just the same, all these years later? This really is preserving history.'

Tony made a few more visits to the museum to check progress and give 'King-Dog' a fond pat, but sadly he never saw the completed project. This was a sharp reminder that tomorrow is often too late.

ERIC BEECHINOR, No. 768 NAS

'The Corsair. Very good, very enjoyable aeroplane.'

We did what seemed like endless airfield dummy deck landings (ADDLs), and I remember being very excited when we finally progressed to real deck landings.

Even after all of our other flying training it was not until I had passed on deck landing that I thought 'right, now I have qualified as a Navy Pilot'.

My first Corsair solo flight – it was at Jacksonville, aged nineteen. It was a powerful experience after flying in Harvards and Vultee Valiants. We all lined up six-abreast on a very wide runway. Then we took off one at a time; this is how our first solo flights were conducted.

I remember one of our men had an engine failure on take-off and crashed into the fuel farm on the edge of the runway. Things could go wrong very quickly.

On one occasion I was coming in to land. I had just made what I thought was a good three-point touchdown and was correcting my line a little with the rudder. Suddenly the rudder pedal slipped away and the aircraft swerved off the tarmac runway and into the soft soil. The rudder pedal on the right-hand side had simple come off, and I had no control. As soon as we had left the runway the aircraft bogged in, lurched forwards and the momentum started a slow forward cartwheel. I could see that the aircraft was going to go right over on to its back.

There was no time to get out. I remember squashing myself down into the seat as far as I could, and hoping that I could keep my head below the armour plate. The aircraft went up and over; I can remember turning off the fuel and switching off the magnetos as we went over, and hoping that I was low enough.

Eric Beechinor, 768 Sqn. *(ΓAAM)*

Corsairs inbound to an unidentified British carrier. With one aircraft safely down, the batsman and Flight Deck Officer have some split-second decisions to make. Following aircraft would be less than 20 seconds away from being committed to land or being signalled to go round again. The airborne Corsair in this picture appears to be going round again. Recovery stations on a busy carrier was a dangerous and testing environment. The fin flash and underwing roundel on the landed Corsair have been modified to South East Asia Command specification, and the FDO is wearing short trousers, locating this scene somewhere in Far Eastern waters. *(FAAM)*

Then, with a tremendous thump, the aircraft was on its back.

It crushed the tail and the top of the cockpit. I was now completely trapped upside down in what remained of the cockpit space. The edge of the cockpit rail was now all but level with the ground; I could just see a glimmer of daylight to one side, in my dark upside-down world.

I gathered my thoughts, unbuckled my straps and started to dig like fury with my hands at the small space where the daylight was showing. I scraped a hole in the soft earth big enough to wriggle through, and remember that I was out and standing by the aeroplane when the emergency wagons arrived.

An inquiry was held, and it transpired that there had been a prior problem with the rudder pedal and that (apparently) the previous pilot to fly the aircraft had made an 'adjustment' using a hammer, with the obvious disastrous consequences.

The armour plate behind the seat definitely saved my life. I suppose that was my worst moment on Corsairs.

PETER LOVEGROVE, No. 768 NAS

*'The Corsair. Good machine, superb to fly.
No real vices, unless you were too slow.
I loved it.'*

I did most of my flying training in Canada, PT-26 Cornells and Harvards, but did not fly a Corsair until I was back in England. By then I had clocked up about 300hr on Harvards so the Corsair was a little easier to get used to.

We were stationed at Zeals [in Wiltshire, England], on a grass airfield. I did my first Corsair solo flight there. We had a thorough technical brief, studied the pilot's notes and did quite a lot of taxying practice. Then off we went.

It was just as they had briefed, a delight to handle. Very powerful, good in formation and combat manoeuvres.

My first deck landing was on to HMS *Ravager*. We were stationed in Scotland by then, at East Haven, and flew out to the ship from there. Sometimes we stayed on board and sometimes we completed our landings and returned to East Haven. Our first deck landings were often the best. You were concentrating so hard and doing it all by the book. The problems started when you had done a few and started to relax. You simply had to follow the batsman's instructions to the letter. You approached the ship in a broad left-hand turn, positioning yourself in what they described as an imaginary cone, spreading out from the stern of the ship. If you could imagine this 'cone' and line yourself up well at this point you were halfway there. The difficult bit was then ignoring your own instincts part-way in to the approach and switching to trusting the batsman's every instruction. Yes, that was the hard part.

The Corsair was a good strong aircraft, it would take a lot of punishment, particularly while you were getting used to deck landing for the first time. I suppose that we all had scary moments. My worst was an intermittent engine failure off the South Coast of England. I returned to base and the engineers checked the aircraft. Six of the lower engine cylinders were dead. I was lucky to get back with that. Also I remember taking off from Eglington, Northern Ireland, only to discover that my air speed indicator was not working. I had no idea what speed I was doing. I radioed in and they diverted me to nearby Maydown Airfield.

The last known and recorded flight of KD431 appears in Peter Lovegrove's FAA flying log book. The date is 7 December 1945.
(Crown copyright/MoD)

YEAR 1945		AIRCRAFT		PILOT, OR 1ST PILOT	2ND PILOT, PUPIL OR PASSENGER	DUTY (INCLUDING RESULTS AND REMARKS)	SINGLE-ENGINE AIRCRA		
							DAY		NIG
							DUAL (1)	PILOT (2)	DUAL (3)
MONTH	DATE	Type	No.						
—		—	—			TOTALS BROUGHT FORWARD	184:25	241:45 237:45	15:30
				R.N.A.S. EASTHAVEN. HMS PEEWIT					
DEC	3	CORSAIR IV	283	SELF		LOCAL FAMIL.			0:35
"	3	CORSAIR III	547	SELF		ADDLS.			0:50
"	4	CORSAIR III	769	SELF		ADDLS.			0:30
"	5	CORSAIR III	769	SELF		ADDLS.			0:15
"	5	CORSAIR III	599	SELF		ADDLS.			0:20
"	7	CORSAIR IV	431	SELF		BASE – H.M.S. RAVAGER – BASE			0:45
"	7	CORSAIR IV	431	SELF		BASE – H.M.S. RAVAGER. 1 DLT.			0:10
"	7	CORSAIR IV	283	SELF		D.L.T.'s 1.			0:40
"	7	CORSAIR IV	283	SELF		D.L.T.'s 3.			0:20
"	11	CORSAIR III	710	SELF		D.L.T.'s 3.			0:45
"	11	CORSAIR III	710	SELF		H.M.S. RAVAGER – BASE.			0:20
				SUMMARY FOR COURSE: D.L.T.	1. CORSAIR.				5:10
				UNIT: 768 Sqd R.N.A.S EASTHAVEN AIRCRAFT	2. LINK.				
				DATE: Dec 10th 1945 TYPES	3. ———				
				SIGNATURE:	4. ———				
			O.d.d.b. Assumed 5. Thirds						
				LT(A) RNVR for C.O. 768 Sqdn.					
					GRAND TOTAL [Cols. (1) to (10)] 465 Hrs. 15 Mins.	TOTALS CARRIED FORWARD	184:25 243:15	241:45	15:30
							(1)	(2)	(3)

Here they had a batsman waiting to guide me in. This was very tricky with no air speed indication in the cockpit. I had to rely more than ever on the batsman's instructions and signals, particularly where my speed was concerned. That was a difficult landing, but it did emphasise just how important the batsman really was.

I remember while we were doing deck landings on HMS *Ravager* there was one Corsair with a broken cockpit canopy. The canopy was stuck in the fully open position. I was detailed to take this aircraft back to East Haven from the ship. It was early December, and I remember it was jolly cold making the forty-minute flight with the hood open all the way!

I suppose we all had our moments, but overall I found the Corsair to be a superb aircraft.

THE LAST DAYS

Peter Lovegrove flew KD431 out to HMS *Ravager* for what he is certain was the aircraft's final deck landing. This took place on 7 December 1945, and was the last series of deck landings performed by No. 768 NAS before the training course came to an end and the squadron disembarked for Christmas leave.

The aircraft did somehow get delivered to the Royal Navy disposal yard at Donibristle, Scotland, early in 1946, and was probably flown there by a ferry pilot. However, Peter remains the last known pilot to have flown the aeroplane, and almost certainly can claim the last deck landing with it.

Postscript

ROLL-OUT 2005

Opposite, top: Roll-out day,
9 August 2005. Fourteen former
Corsair pilots line up in front of
KD431 to mark the occasion.
Left to right: Tony Maylett, Peter
Jupe, Chris Clark, Gordon
Dunnell, Dennis White, Eric
Beechinor, Donald MacQueen,
Peter Lovegrove, Alan Leahy,
Peter Howell, Harry Greenup,
Daniel Earp, Don Attenburrow,
and John Taylor. *(FAAM)*

On 9 August 2005 KD431 was rolled out of the restoration hangar and placed back on display in the Second World War exhibition hall at the FAAM. To mark the occasion, fourteen former FAA Corsair pilots attended the ceremony, and all agreed that this project had been the correct treatment for KD431. Their applause to the restoration team clearly signified their feelings and understanding that the last FAA Corsair had been saved in original condition.

Present for the occasion, and meeting for the very first time, were Chris Clark and Peter Lovegrove, respectively the first and last pilots to fly KD431. It is difficult to imagine a more fitting way to conclude the project.

Right: Chris Clark (cockpit), the
first person to fly KD431, meets
Peter Lovegrove, the last known
pilot of the aircraft. They met for
the first time at the roll-out
ceremony to mark the
completion of KD431's
restoration, and had much to
talk about at this unique event.
They are now very good friends.
(FAAM)

Opposite, bottom: As part of the
roll-out ceremony, the pilots
were presented with a picture of
KD431, which they all signed for
each other, to keep as a
memento of the day. *(Harry
Dempsey Graphics)*

ROYAL NAVY
KD 431

E2 ⊙ M

Appendix I

CORSAIR TECHNICAL DATA

F4U-1 (British Mk I); F4U-1A and F4U-1D (British Mk II)

Manufacturer
Chance Vought Aircraft Company, Stratford, Connecticut, USA
Type
Single-seat, carrier-borne fighter/fighter-bomber

F3A-1 (British Mk III)

Manufacturer
Brewster Aeronautical Corporation, Johnsville, Pennsylvania, USA
(parent company, Brewster Aeronautical Corporation, Long Island, New York, USA)

FG-1A and FG-1D (British Mk IV)

Manufacturer
Goodyear Aircraft Company, Akron, Ohio, USA
Wingspan: 41ft 0in
Royal Navy clipped-wing version: 39ft 8in
Length: 34ft 5in
Height: 15ft 1in
Weight: Mk I, II & III, 8,800lb (empty); Mk IV, 9,100lb (empty)
Engines: Mk I, II & III, Pratt & Whitney R-2800-8 Double Wasp; Mk IV, Pratt & Whitney R-2800-8W Double Wasp
Performance: Mk. I, II & III, maximum speed 375mph at 2,000hp; Mk IV, maximum speed 415mph at 2,250hp
Armament: Mk I, II, III & early Mk IV, six fixed 0.50in machine-guns in wings. Provision for one central bomb mount; later Mk IV, two wing-pylon bombs

Opposite: The basic dimensions of Goodyear-built Corsairs, taken from the maintenance and rigging manual. The manual depicts the US Navy Corsair, not the clipped-wing British variant. *(Goodyear Tire & Rubber)*

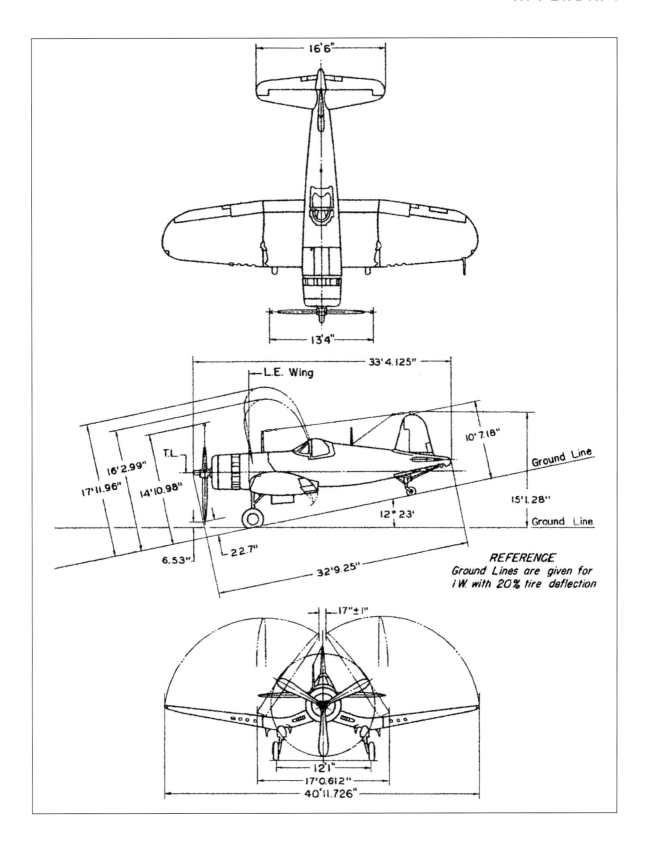

16'6"

13'4"

33'4.125"

L.E. Wing

10' 7.18"

Ground Line

T.L.

16'2.99"

17'11.96"

14'10.98"

15'1.28"

Ground Line

12° 23'

6.53"

2.2.7"

32'9.25"

REFERENCE
Ground Lines are given for
I.W. with 20% tire deflection

17" ± 1"

12'1"

17'0.612"

40'11.726"

Appendix II

CORSAIR KD431 – A DIARY OF KNOWN DATES AND MOVEMENTS

1944

Mid-July
On production line at Goodyear factory. Akron, Ohio, USA.

22 August
First test flight, Goodyear factory, Akron, Ohio. Pilot C.J. Clarke. *(Log book)*

23 August
Second test flight. Goodyear factory, Akron, Ohio. Pilot C.J. Clarke. *(Log book)*

October/November
Delivered to Lockheed, Renfrew, Glasgow, Scotland.

8 November
Transferred to No. 23 Maintenance Unit (MU), Aldergrove, Northern Ireland.

1945

14 January
Test flown at No. 23 MU, Aldergrove. Pilot Flt Lt Harry Clarke, RAF. *(Log book)*

15 January
Flown to No 48. MU, Hawarden, North Wales. Pilot First Officer Graham, Air Transport Auxiliary. *(Log book)*

16 January
Continued flight to Stretton, Royal Naval Aircraft Yard. *(Aldergrove dispatch log book)*

June
First reference of being on 1835 Sqn, Eglinton, County Londonderry, Northern Ireland, coded 'S' (in white).

29 July
Deck landing training, HMS *Premier*; K.A.S. Mitchell. *(Log book)*

31 July
Loaded on to HMS *Patroller* at Sydenham Docks, destined for Far East. During this week the code letters may have been changed to blue from white and the gas patch applied.

7–8 August
Unloaded from HMS *Patroller*. Hostilities ended, did not sail.

September
Joined 768 Sqn at RNAS Ballyhalbert, Northern Ireland. Flying on to HMS *Premier* for deck-landing training.

27 September
Deck-landing practice, HMS *Premier*. Pilot E. Beechinor. *(Log book)*

27 September
Barrier accident on HMS *Premier*. Pilot J.D.P. Foulkes.

28 September
Flown again after repair.

October
Still with 768 Sqn. Now operating from RNAS East Haven, Scotland. Aircraft coded E2-M (in white). Deck-landing training on HMS *Ravager*.

7 December
Last known deck-landing flight. Pilot Peter Lovegrove. *(Log book)*
(Early in 1946 transferred to Donibristle, Fifeshire, for disposal.)

1946

20 May
Invitation for Cranfield College to inspect for suitability. *(Admiralty memo)*

23 May

Confirmation of suitability. *(Cranfield letter)*

(At some time between 23 May and 3 July 1946, aircraft delivered to Cranfield by road.)

3 July

At Cranfield and assembled. *(Cranfield memo)*

1963

February

Approval for transfer to FAAM. *(Admiralty memo)*

June

Displayed at Yeovilton Air Day. (Post-Air Day, June 1963 KD431 transferred into the care of the FAAM.

1999

November

Moved to FAAM restoration hangar for inspection work.

2000

January

Project begins to remove 1963 paint, retaining the 1944 paint.

2005

April

Work completed.

9 August

Roll-out ceremony to return aircraft to display in FAAM.

Appendix III

CORSAIR SQUADRONS OF THE FLEET AIR ARM

First- and second-line FAA squadrons equipped with Corsairs during the Second World War (and immediately postwar). It should be noted that second-line squadrons may have operated limited numbers of Corsairs among their other complements of aircraft, and that No. 885 NAS normally operated Grumman Hellcats and Avengers at this time, but was equipped with Corsairs for a short time during 1945.

	Front-line Sqns	Second-line Sqns
Corsair F4U-1 (Mk I)	1830	700
	1831	732
	1833	738
	1834	787
	1835	
	1836	
	1837	
	1838	
	1841	
	1848	
Corsair F4U-1A (Mk II)	1830	703
Corsair F4U-1D (Mk II)	1833	706
	1834	723
	1835	731
	1836	732
	1837	738
	1838	748
	1841	757
	1842	768
	1843	771

	Front-line Sqns	Second-line Sqns
	1848	778
	885	787
Corsair F3A-1 (Mk III)	1835	700
	1837	715
	1841	718
	1842	719
	1843	731
	1845	736
	1846	748
	1849	757
		759
		760
		767
		768
		771
		778
		787
		794
Corsair FG-1A (Mk IV)		
Corsair FG-1D (Mk IV)	1831	706
	1834	715
	1835	718
	1836	721
	1841	733
	1842	757
	1843	759
	1845	767
	1846	768
	1849	778
	1850	787
	1851	791
	1852	794
	1853	
	885	

Appendix IV

SOME OF THE RESTORATION TECHNIQUES USED ON KD431

The following is a list of basic techniques discovered, experimented with and used on KD431 during the paint-removal process. This is a guide only, and it must be emphasised that variations in technique occurred at almost every stage of working. The process was affected by panel shape, panel contour, paint thickness, paint type, colour, condition of undersurface, temperature changes and light conditions.

TECHNIQUE 1

Enamel paint (now flaking in areas) applied to factory-applied cellulose paint finish can be successfully removed by careful picking and scraping using a scalpel and/or plastic scraper. Any light scratches or graze marks caused by this work could be polished smooth using automotive rubbing compound, gently applied with 0000-grade cabinetmaker's finishing wire wool, and polished to a finish with finer grades of rubbing compound and a clean rag.

TECHNIQUE 2

Emulsion paint applied over factory-applied black propeller finish can be successfully removed by gently rubbing the area with white spirit applied using white Scotchbrite-type wadding.

TECHNIQUE 3

Cellulose paint applied to another unprepared or abraded paint finish can, with care and patience, be removed using metal polish wadding to rub away the top finish, leaving the under-finish exposed. This can be polished to a finish using fine-grade rubbing compound, and finally finished by the application of a wax polish.

TECHNIQUE 4

If paint finishes that have been applied on to another unprepared top coat are proving stubborn to remove, they can be VERY CAREFULLY removed using cellulose or acrylic thinners. Carefully applied using rag, soft white Scotchbrite wadding or very fine cabinetmaker's wire wool, this will remove successive layers of paint in a controlled manner.

WARNING: there is a health and safety issue here regarding flammable liquids, adequate ventilation, inhalation prevention, and eye and skin protection. Furthermore, this technique requires great skill and practice. The success rate is good with practice and care, but no guarantee can be made. IT IS NOT EASY, AND DISASTERS CAN OCCUR. Anyone thinking of using this method is strongly advised to practise on a sufficient number of test pieces first. If in doubt, do not risk the object. Repeat; DO NOT RISK THE OBJECT.

TECHNIQUE 5

Some areas of polyurethane paint can be removed from the original cellulose paint by using low-tack double-sided adhesive tape. This is only possible where the underlayer of cellulose paint is in very sound condition, and where the polyurethane paint is becoming friable and detached. On the Corsair this worked best on the wing roundel details, particularly where the cellulose paint had soaked into the fabric area of the wing surface, providing a particularly sound key. This method can result in a disaster at any given time, and must be limited to areas having very sound under-paint surfaces, and to small areas so as to maintain control. Small test pieces are essential to prove the technique in any given area. If in doubt, DO NOT TRY IT!

Appendix V

SURVIVING CORSAIRS

Between forty and fifty substantially complete Corsairs currently survive throughout the world, in museums or with private collectors. Some are static museum examples, and many are still airworthy and regularly flown. Numerous listings of these aircraft appear on various websites and databases, and due to many factors (changes of ownership, rebuilds, damage and original database flaws) it is almost impossible to create a listing that is not out of date the minute it is completed. This listing is intended to provide a general indication of surviving Corsair numbers as of 2005. The accompanying information is not guaranteed complete, and if an aeroplane has been omitted, please accept the author's apologies and write to him at the FAAM.

(**Key:** CV = Chance Vought; GY = Goodyear; BR = Brewster)

Maker	Type	Serial No. (civil registration)	Bureau No.	Owner/comments
GY	FG-1A	KD431	14862	FAA Museum, England
GY	FG-1A	Not known	13459	USMC Museum, California, USA
CV	F4U-1A	(NX83782)	17799	Planes of Fame Museum, USA
CV	F4U-1A	NZ2501	17995	New Zealand Fighter Pilots' Museum, Wanaka, New Zealand
GY	FG-1D	NZ5648	92044	NZFPM, Wanaka, New Zealand
GY	FG-1D	(G-BXUL)	88391	Old Flying Machine Company, Duxford, England
GY	FG-1D	(G-FGID)	88297	Louis Antonacci, USA
GY	FG-1D	(N11Y)	67087	C&C Air Corp, USA
GY	FG-1D	(G-CCMV)	92399	Not known
GY	FG-1D	(N83JC)	67089	Jeff Clyman, USA
GY	FG-1D	(N9964Z)	92468	Commemorative Air Force, USA
GY	FG-1D	Not known	Not known	A. Mcdonnell, USA

GY	FG-1D	(N3PP)	92509	Kalamazoo Air Museum, USA
GY	FG-1D	(N72NW)	92436	B. Reynolds, USA(?)
GY	FG-1D	(NX773RD)	92433	R. Dieckman, USA
GY	FG-1D	(N194G)	92050	J. Axtell(?), USA
GY	FG-1D	(N3466G)	92132	B. Schroeder, USA
GY	FG-1D	Not known	88382	Museum of Flight, Seattle, USA
GY	FG-1D	(N67HP)	92095	D. Smith, Oregon, USA
GY	FG-1D	(N62290)	92629	B. Pond, USA
GY	FG-1D	(N766JD)	92246	US Naval Aviation Museum (NAM), Pensacola, Florida, USA
GY	FG-1D	—	88368	USS Yorktown Museum, USA
GY	FG-1D	(NX106FG)	92106	G. Kohs, Michigan, USA
GY	F2G-1	(NX5588N)	88457	R. Odegaard, USA
CV	F4U-4	(N68HP)	97302	H. Pardue, USA
CV	F4U-4	(NX72378)	97388	G. Beck, USA
CV	F4U-4	(N713JT)	97143	J. Tobul, USA
CV	F4U-4	(N3771A)	97142	Pima Air Museum, USA
CV	F4U-4	(NX53JB)	81698	J. MacGuire, USA
CV	F4U-4	(NX6667)	97259	Experimental Aircraft Assoc., USA
CV	F4U-4	(N4802X)	97349	NAM, Pensacola, Florida, USA
CV	F4U-4	(N5215V)	97286	K. Weeks, USA
CV	F4U-4	(N5222V)	97330	Bootstrap Aircraft, USA
CV	F4U-4	(OE-EAS)	96995	S. Angerer, Austria
CV	F4U-4B	(N47991)	97390	C. Nichols, USA
CV	F4U-4B	(NX240CA)	97142	M. Chapman, USA
CV	F4U-5N	(N65WF)	122184	J. Smith, USA
CV	F4U-5N	(N43RW)	121881	Lone Star Museum, USA
CV	F4U-5N	(N179PT)	122179	J. Read, USA
CV	F4U-5N	FAH609	124715	Museo del Aire, Honduras
CV	F4U-5NL	(N4901W)	124569	R. Thompson, USA
CV	F4U-5NL	(N49068)	124486	M. George, USA
CV	F4U-5NL	Not known	122189	USMC Museum, California, USA
CV	F4U-5NL	(N100CV)	124447	Mid-America Air Museum, Kansas, USA
BR	F3A-1	Not known	04634	L. Cralley, USA*

*Although this is not a complete aircraft, it is worth recording, as it is the only known substantial surviving portion of a Brewster-built Corsair.

Bibliography

PRIMARY SOURCES – DOCUMENTARY

FLEET AIR ARM MUSEUM ARCHIVES

Aircraft accident record (A25) card index
Aircraft photographic files
Corsair aircraft information file for KD431
Fleet Air Arm squadron record and line books
Fleet Air Arm pilots' flying log books (K.A.S. Mitchell, E. Beechinor,
    P. Lovegrove, H. Clarke, RAF)
Flight log book of First Officer C.J. Graham (former ATA delivery pilot)
Flight log book of C. Clarke (former Goodyear test pilot)
Flight dispatch log, No. 23 Maintenance Unit (MU), Aldergrove, Northern
    Ireland

Royal Naval Aircraft Serviceability Form, FONAS Form 59, August 1943
CAFO 618 A01443/43 – 5 April 1945
CAFO 619 A/AWD2783/44 –5 April 1945
CAFO 1099 A/AWD670/45 – June 1945
Naval stores document NS 0106/38-31.8.39

GOODYEAR AIRCRAFT CORPORATION ARCHIVE
Copy of Goodyear Aircraft Build Fabrication Log GER 2569
Corsair F4U-1 series technical data, rigging and repair manual

PRIMARY SOURCES – ORAL HISTORY INTERVIEWS

Eric Beechinor, Bob Beers, Douglas Buchanan, Charlie Carter, Chris Clark,
Harry Clarke, Stan Deeley, Bill Fisher, John Foulkes, Hubert Hartley, Nick
Hauprich, Cdr R.C. Hay DSO, DSC & Bar, Cdr L. Hooke, Elizabeth

Horsford, Peter Jupe, Peter Lovegrove, Lt Cdr D. MacQueen, Tony Mitchell, John Morton, John Taylor, Ray Wills, Lavinia Woodbine-Parish

SECONDARY SOURCES – PUBLISHED BOOKS

Guyton, B.T. *Whistling Death*, Atglen, PA, Schiffer Publishing, 1994

O'Leary, M. *Fighting Corsairs*, Canoga Park, CA, War Eagle Publications, 1984

O'Leary, M. *United States Naval Fighters of World War II in Action*, Poole, Blandford Press, 1980

Sturtivent, R. and Balance, T. *Squadrons of the Fleet Air Arm*, Tunbridge Wells, Air-Britain (Historians), 1994

Sturtivent, R. and Burrow, M. *Fleet Air Arm Aircraft 1939–45*, Tunbridge Wells, Air-Britain (Historians), 1995

Sullivan, J. *F4U Corsair in Action*, Carrollton, TX, Squadron/Signal Publications, 1994

Thetford, O. *British Naval Aircraft Since 1912*, London, Putnam, 1982

Thomas, G.J. *Eyes for The Phoenix*, Aldershot, Hikoki Publications, 1999

NEWSPAPERS

Blanchard, M.P. 'End Nears for a Plant That Made Flying Junk', *Philadelphia Inquirer* (15 July 2001), p. A01

Hinson, P. 'Hello, Hello, Hello – and Who's Behind This Then?' *Cranfield Express,* 18 (September 2001), p. 1

Index